DPO Handbook

Data Protection Officers Under the GDPR

Thomas J. Shaw, Esq.

© 2018 Thomas J. Shaw
Published by the International Association of Privacy Professionals (IAPP)

All rights reserved. No part of this publication may be reproduced, stored in a retrieval system or transmitted in any form or by any means, mechanical, photocopying, recording or otherwise, without the prior, written permission of the publisher, International Association of Privacy Professionals, Pease International Tradeport, 75 Rochester Ave., Suite 4, Portsmouth, NH 03801, United States of America.

Nothing contained in this book is to be considered as the rendering of legal advice for specific cases, and readers are responsible for obtaining such advice from their own legal counsel. This book is intended for educational and informational purposes only.

Copy editor and Proofreader: Joni McNeal

ISBN: 978-1-948771-04-7

Contents

Foreword . . . . *vii*
Dedication . . . . *xi*
Acronyms Used . . . . *xiii*
About the Author . . . . *xv*

Chapter 1: Introduction to the DPO Role
    1.1 Is a DPO Required? 2
        1.1.1 GDPR — Mandatory and Voluntary DPOs 2
        1.1.2 DPO Role — What Are Organizations Thinking? 4
    1.2 The Skills and Professions Of a DPO 8
        1.2.1 DPO Skills 8
        1.2.2 DPO Professions 14

Chapter 2: Initiating the DPO Role
    2.1 Defining the Role and Outsourcing 22
        2.1.1 Defining the Role 22
        2.1.2 Outsourcing 26
    2.2 First Tasks of the DPO 35
        2.2.1 Start-Up Tasks 35
        2.2.2 Data Protection Policy and Data and Processing Inventory 39

Chapter 3: DPO Tasks — GDPR Compliance
    3.1 GDPR Compliance — Controllers and Processors 46
        3.1.1 Data Processing Obligations 47
        3.1.2 Data Subject Rights 55
        3.1.3 Security and Breach 60
        3.1.4 Other Obligations 63
        3.1.5 Other Statutes 65

  3.1.6 Processors under the GDPR....................................67

  3.1.7 Processor — Controller Agreement 69

 3.2 GDPR Compliance — Assessments, Audits, Certifications 70

  3.2.1 GDPR Compliance High-Level Checklist and Questions 71

  3.2.2 GDPR Initial Assessment and Audits 74

  3.2.3 Certification under GDPR and Codes of Conduct.................77

Chapter 4: DPO Tasks — Risk and DPIAs

 4.1 Risk..82

  4.1.1 ISO 27005 83

  4.1.2 Risk in the GDPR..92

 4.2 Data Protection Impact Assessments 94

  4.2.1 GDPR 95

  4.2.2 Methodologies 98

Chapter 5: DPO Tasks — Technical Assessments

 5.1 Information Security and Anonymization...........................106

  5.1.1 ISO 107

  5.1.2 NIST 112

  5.1.3 Anonymization 115

 5.2 Data Breach and Privacy by Design 117

  5.2.1 Data Breach 118

  5.2.2 Privacy by Design and Default 127

Chapter 6: DPO Tasks — Outside the EU

 6.1 Transferring Data Outside the EU 138

  6.1.1 Adequacy and Derogations 138

  6.1.2 SCCs and BCRs 141

 6.2 Non-EU Controllers and Privacy Laws..............................143

  6.2.1 Controllers Not in the EU 144

  6.2.2 Other Countries' Privacy Laws 148

Chapter 7: Putting It All Together — Example Scenarios

    7.1 Leaping Unicorns Ltd. — SME 156

        7.1.1 Leaping Unicorn's Situation 156

        7.1.2 Introducing/Initiating the DPO Role 157

        7.1.3 Assessing GDPR Compliance 158

        7.1.4 Technical Assessments 162

        7.1.5 Data Transfers 163

    7.2 Exhilarating Elephants Inc. — Multinational 165

        7.2.1 Exhilarating Elephants' Situation 165

        7.2.2 Introducing/Initiating the DPO Role 166

        7.2.3 Assessing GDPR Compliance 167

        7.2.4 Technical Assessments 172

        7.2.5 Data Transfers 175

Appendix A: Various Topics for DPOs

    Outsourcing Your DPO: Real-Life Scenarios 179

        Vulnerability Testing 179

        Photographic Images 180

        Unified Consent 181

        App Developer. 182

    Subject Access Requests Under the GDPR — Uses in Litigation. 183

    Legal Response to Data Breaches in the Cloud 186

    Consent to Children's Data — Is It Legal? 190

        The Law. 191

        The Forms 192

        Conclusion 193

    EU Data Transfers to the U.S. — Model Clauses but Why? 194

Appendix B: Table of Authorities

    Cases 199

    Statutes 199

    Guidance 200

    Standards 203

    Opinions. 204

Foreword

This book arises out of a series of articles I wrote about and experiences I have had in the role of data protection officer (DPO) under the EU's new General Data Protection Regulation (GDPR). While the GDPR has mandated this role in certain circumstances and at a high level specified the tasks that must be performed, it has left much unsaid. The Article 29 Data Protection Working Party (WP29) of EU data protection authorities has tried to provide some guidance, but many key questions about how to perform the role remain. This book is an attempt to fill these gaps and explain to a new DPO how to perform their role.

It is important to understand that this book is written as a manual of first impression, based upon the author's experiences in this industry across the world for the last three decades. However, the book is being written about a new role under a new legal statute that is only now coming into force. No one really has any experience with this role under this statute. As such, some interpretations must be made on a projected trajectory that will be recalibrated as DPOs gain experience under this new regulation. As such, I expect there to be frequent and perhaps substantial revisions to this book as time goes on and very much welcome constructive input from those in the profession about topics needing more clarity or focus.

It is also important to understand that this book is written by referring to two other related books by the author that have deeper explanations for those who wish to acquire such knowledge. While this book has the essential information to perform the DPO role, these two other books will greatly enhance the DPO's knowledge and ability to perform their role. The first is *Information and Internet Law — Global Practice* for those wanting to understand all the privacy, information security, data breach, cybercrime, messaging, surveillance, internet access and content, e-commerce, and online intellectual property laws around the world.

The second is *Emerging Technologies Law — Global Practice* for those wanting to understand the legal issues surrounding more than 30 emerging technologies from a global perspective, from social media, mobile computing, and cloud computing to robots, drones, blockchains, 3D printing, virtual currencies, augmented reality, artificial intelligence, and the internet of things. Both books are referenced throughout this book when further knowledge is important.

The audience for this book is anyone who undertakes the DPO role under the GDPR. This includes those who take on the role full time or part time, those who are hired into the role or who move laterally into it, those who are taking it on in addition to other organizational functions or for whom it is the only role, those who are in the private sector or government, and those who are doing it as an employee of a company or as an outsourced service provider. There is no specific training or profession that this book applies to, as whomever an organization determines to be qualified to be a DPO is the target audience.

The intended use of this book is to provide an overall guide to new and experienced DPOs to fulfill their role from a high level. There are specifics of each situation, industry, system, and technology that require customization by the DPO to perform their role. In addition, this is not a legal guide that addresses any specific case. DPOs should first read the GDPR in detail for the needed clarity, and if that is not sufficient, then legal guidance should be sought from an appropriate lawyer. The same applies to being able to audit various aspects of systems that are required to be compliant. If the DPO cannot find sufficient evidence to support compliance, audit guidance should be sought from an appropriate audit professional.

This book was written in a relatively short period of time to ensure its availability before the GDPR comes into force. As such, it may temporarily contain errors or omissions that I would ask readers to kindly notify me of. Also, while the specifics of the GDPR are covered, for each rule there are many exceptions and qualifications. These may apply to only a smaller number of situations and as such are not discussed herein. The goal is to deal with the vast majority of situations DPOs encounter. Certain areas are not covered, such as data about criminal justice or member state statutes and restrictions.

While this book is naturally written within the EU focusing on EU law, I have tried to bring a global perspective. Having lived and worked outside the United States for the last quarter century in all three parts of the global triad while practicing across many related disciplines, I have tried to bring a global viewpoint and multidisciplinary approach to this discussion of international statutes, cases, and guidance. DPOs will not only be based in the EU but also located globally. The law that DPOs will need to deal with is not only the GDPR but their local privacy laws.

The chapters in order cover whether a DPO is required and the skills and professions are best suited for the role; structuring and initiating the DPO role; GDPR compliance for controllers and processors; understanding risk and data protection impact assessments; technical assessments DPOs are involved with for information security, data breach response, and privacy by design; the mechanisms for transferring personal data outside the EEA and when controllers, processors, or DPOs operate outside the EU; and two example scenarios of a DPO in action using these varied techniques. An Appendix contains articles that would be of interest to a DPO.

A brief word about the cover image for this book. It was designed to reflect the four principal stakeholders a DPO is responsive to: the board of directors/highest levels of management, the business/support units of controllers and processors, data protection supervisory authorities, and data subjects who contact DPOs directly. Behind those are other legs representing the principal tasks of the DPO: to advise, inform, monitor, and cooperate.

I intend for this book to be regularly updated with the experiences of DPOs as they begin to operate under the GDPR from May 2018. Some of the practical advice should be seen as initial efforts at guidance that leaves lots of room to be supplemented by methodologies that are most familiar or helpful to the DPO. Everyone may have certain audit techniques or interview methodologies that work the best for them. DPOs should feel free to substitute their favored practices as appropriate. I would ask that they share those techniques for future editions of this book to create an improving best practices handbook for all DPOs working under the GDPR.

Thomas J. Shaw, Esq.
February 2018

Dedication

No one can write a book without the support of those who make up the panoramas and portraits of their daily lives and loves. I wish again, in this my ninth book, to express my gratitude to my wife and daughter and to our much beloved companion now in her 16th year of hilarity, harmony, and huskiness.

Acronyms Used

There are many acronyms used throughout the book that should become second nature to a data protection officer.

GDPR	General Data Protection Regulation
DPD	Data Protection Directive
InfoSec	information security (often called just "security")
DPO	data protection officer
DPIA	data protection impact assessment
PIA	privacy impact assessment
DPA	data protection authority (called Supervisory Authority in the GDPR)
DS	data subject
DPC	Data Protection Commissioner (Ireland)
ICO	Information Commissioner's Office (U.K.)
CNIL	Commission Nationale de l'Informatique et des Libertés (France)
IPC	Information and Privacy Commissioner (Ontario)
WP29	Article 29 Working Party (under DPD)
ISO	International Standards Organization
ISP	internet (or intermediary) service provider
EC	European Commission
ENISA	EU Agency for Network and Information Security
EDPB	European Data Protection Board (under GDPR)
PbD	privacy by design
PII	personally identifiable information
PKI	public key infrastructure

About the Author

Thomas J. Shaw, Esq., is a EU-based attorney at law, CPA, CIPP/E, CIPP/US, CRISC, ECM^M, CISM, ERM^P, CISA, CGEIT and CCSK, assistant professor of information, internet and emerging technologies law lecturing at leading universities in the EU, editor/founder of the American Bar Association's *Information Law Journal* and its antecedents, and the author of the following books on global technology law and legal history:

- *DPO Handbook — Data Protection Officers under the GDPR*
- *Emerging Technologies Law — Global Practice*
- *Information and Internet Law — Global Practice*
- *World War I Law and Lawyers — Issues, Cases, and Characters*
- *Cloud Computing for Lawyers and Executives — A Global Approach, Second edition*
- *World War II Law and Lawyers — Issues, Cases, and Characters*
- *Children and the Internet — A Global Guide for Lawyers and Parents*
- *Cloud Computing for Lawyers and Executives — A Global Approach*
- *Information Security and Privacy — A Practical Guide for Global Executives, Lawyers and Technologists*

He can be reached at thomas@tshawlaw.com.

CHAPTER 1

Introduction to the DPO Role

It is new, but, like a rediscovered friend or lost photo found, seems so familiar. The data protection officer (DPO) role is part of the General Data Protection Regulation (GDPR), which commences May 25, 2018. The role is made up of new requirements that are not part of current practice, new requirements that mandate what was previously optional, and still more that have been part of best practice for a long time. This newly synthesized function is one that may require re-evaluating how the role, if currently filled, is staffed and carried out, but in any situation, needs a fresh perspective on the duties involved and skills required.

The DPO role is not mandatory under the GDPR unless certain types of conditions exist, so the first step is for an organization to analyze whether a DPO is required. A DPO can be engaged because they are required or can be brought on voluntarily, but, in either case, there is a series of tasks the DPO must perform. Knowing those tasks, the next step is to determine the type of job skills that someone in the DPO role should have to be able to succeed in this position. Certification based on those skills and experiences may help with this. A further step is to decide which profession to look to find most, if not all, these skills. In these early days, it is helpful to know what other organizations are doing or planning for their DPO role.

DPO Areas of Focus

- Whether a DPO is required or optional
- What other organizations are doing
- Skills required of a DPO and DPO certifications
- Appropriate professions for a DPO

1.1 Is a DPO Required?

The first question for organizations is to determine whether they need a DPO. The role may be required under law, or the organization may determine it would be in their best interest to staff this position. There are more clearly defined criteria for the legally mandated analysis, while the voluntary decision analysis is more subjective. Whether the DPO is to be established or not, the analysis and conclusions must be documented by the respective controller or processor engaging the DPO. Because the GDPR[1] is still in its early days, what other organizations are thinking and doing provides useful insight and helps underline some of the important characteristics of the DPO role. To gain this knowledge, a survey was sent out via privacy and DPO organizations to their members.

1.1.1 GDPR — Mandatory and Voluntary DPOs

Under Article 37, the GDPR specifies that a DPO is required to be appointed by a controller or processor in the following situations:

- The processing is carried out by a public authority or body, except for courts acting in their judicial capacity.
- The core activities of the controller or the processor consist of processing operations which, by virtue of their nature, their scope and/or their purposes, require regular and systematic monitoring of data subjects on a large scale.

---

[1] Regulation (EU) 2016/679 of the European Parliament and of the Council of 27 April 2016 on the protection of natural persons with regard to the processing of personal data and on the free movement of such data, and repealing Directive 95/46/EC (General Data Protection Regulation).

- The core activities of the controller or the processor consist of processing on a large scale of special categories of data pursuant to Article 9 and personal data relating to criminal convictions and offences referred to in Article 10."

The WP29 has published guidance to further explain these requirements.[2] All public authorities would be expected to designate a DPO, but the WP29 noted that private organizations sometimes may carry out public tasks or exercise public authority in areas such as public transportation, utilities, infrastructure, housing, and broadcasting. These organizations are not required to nominate a DPO, yet they are encouraged to do so given data subjects have little choice over having their data processed by such organizations.

"Core activities" are those that encompass how an organization makes money and an activity supporting the money-making processes. The WP29 cited the use of health data by a hospital as being part of its core activities of providing health care services, as opposed to support activities, like human resources, accounting, or IT, that all organizations would use. "Large scale" is not defined in the GDPR, but factors to consider include the number of data subjects involved, the volume of data, the different types of data, the permanence of the processing, and the geographic scope of the processing. Hospitals, banks, insurance companies, telecom providers, and ISPs were cited as large-scale processors in the normal course of their businesses.

"Regular and systematic monitoring" is defined to include but not be limited to online tracking and profiling, including tracking used for behavioral advertising. The "regular" aspect can be ongoing, occurring at regular intervals, or continuous, while systematic would take plan as part of a pre-arranged according to plan to gather data to achieve a strategy. Telecom services, email and data-driven marketing, profiling and scoring, location tracking, behavioral advertising, CCTV, wearable device monitoring, and smart connected devices, including those comprising the internet of things[3] are all considered to be undertaking regular and systematic monitoring.

When an organization does not strictly meet one of these mandated situations, the WP29 believes it is still beneficial to appoint a DPO

---

2 Art. 29 DP WP, Guidelines on Data Protection Officers ("DPOs") (Apr. 2017).
3 *See* Thomas J. Shaw, *Emerging Technologies Law — Global Practice*.

voluntarily, given the assistance the role provides in complying with the new regulation and the significant increase in creditability with data subjects and DPAs. In either case, the decision to have to have a DPO or not must then be documented, citing the factors listed above in concluding with the role is required or not and whether voluntary designation will occur. The GDPR requires that a DPO appointed under a voluntary designation has all the same tasks and controllers have the same obligations for the DPO as if the role was required.

1.1.2 DPO Role — What Are Organizations Thinking?

Another way to get a feel for the need for a DPO is to query organizations. This provides an understanding of how others are viewing the DPO role under the GDPR, especially those who are currently in data protection roles responsible for compliance with existing laws under the DPD.[4] To achieve this, a survey was disseminated through both the IAPP and the Irish national association of DPOs to their membership. This survey asked people to answer questions about their organization's plans regarding the DPO role under the GDPR. Although probably not statistically meaningful as the total responses totaled several dozen, the answers may shed some light on EU organizations' current thinking and introduces some of the requirements for the DPO role, which will be expanded on in the next section and next chapter.

1.1.2.1 The Survey

The survey asked 10 questions, variously posed as yes/no, multiple choice, and fill-in-the-box answers. The final two questions dealt with the respondent organization's industry and their roles under the GDPR as either a data controller or processor. The industries that the organizations represented were broadly across the spectrum, including health, education, finance, retail, broadcasting, software development, IT, human resources, communications, hospitality, transportation, electronics, and national and local government. The data protection roles undertaken by the organizations under the GDPR and the DPD were as a data controller, data processor, or, in the majority of cases, organizations were acting as both controller and processor.

---

4 Directive 95/46/EC of the European Parliament and of the Council of 24 October 1995 on the protection of individuals with regard to the processing of personal data and on the free movement of such data (DPD).

The other eight substantive questions and their responses were as follows:

- Will your organization require a different skill set for the DPO role under the GDPR than it does for its current DPO? Most of the responses answered "yes" that a different skill set will be required in the future, while only a few believed "no" that a different skill set will not be required. However, the second most common answer was that the organization does not currently have someone in a DPO role, which is to be expected given it is not part of the DPD.

- How will your DPO meet the strict requirements for independence under the GDPR (Article 37(1))? The responses were varied, which included meeting the independence requirement through a separation of duties or express contract terms, by the DPO reporting directly to the CEO of the organization, by reporting only to the legal department, or by the DPO role being outsourced. Other responses found organizations will achieve independence through the use of an independent contractor, while others already viewed their DPO role as independent, were not sure if the DPO would be independent, or were still trying to determine how to answer this requirement. Access to independent legal counsel and a separate budget were cited as techniques to ensure independence.

- How will your DPO avoid conflict of interests as specified by the GDPR (Article 38(6))? Some respondents found that potential conflicts of interests were addressed through outsourcing the DPO role, while others thought there were already sufficient conflict of interest rules in place within their organization. Some responses said that with the DPO function being the sole role this person would engage in should be a sufficient control to avoid conflicts of interest, while others were not yet sure how the DPO would avoid conflicts of interest or felt it was up to the personal and professional qualities of the DPO themselves. Even when avoiding conflicts of interests, concerns were cited for possible conflicts with the DPO's attention and resources.

Other respondents believed that spending most of their time on DPO tasks or reporting to the legal department would prevent a conflict of interest. Lawyer legal ethics requirements were cited as a way to prevent conflicts, as was limiting the decision power of DPOs to personal data decisions, as adequate training and a separate budget.

- Will your DPO report directly to the board of directors as specified by the GDPR (Article 38(3))? The vast majority of the respondents agreed that the DPO in their organization would report to the highest level in their organization, with only a small percent not having this type of reporting line. The latter presumably will regularly issue reports to the board instead of having a direct reporting line.

- Will your DPO, required by the GDPR to have expert knowledge of data protection law (Articles 37(1) and 37(5)), be a privacy lawyer, an auditor, a compliance specialist, an IT specialist, a non-technical manager, or from some other profession? The variety of professions specified in the responses were broad. The question choices presented as possible answers included an auditor, compliance specialist, IT specialist, privacy lawyer, non-technical manager, and other (fill in the box). The largest number of professions listed (the question allowed for multiple answers) was for non-technical manager, compliance specialist, privacy lawyer, and IT specialist. Professions specified in the other category included risk specialist, records manager, administrative person, and business manager, with one specifying a combination of manager, compliance specialist, and auditor with a budget for outside legal counsel.

- How many years of professional experience will your DPO have? The respondents to this question, unlike many of the DPO hiring advertisements being posted online, looked to a very experienced professional. The number of years of the DPO ranged from five and seven years to 30 and more than 30 years of experience, with the most common answer 15 years. Only a few responses thought that the DPO role could be filled with an inexperienced resource.

- Will your DPO role be filled by one person or more than one person? Three-fourths of the respondents believed that a single person would fulfil the DPO role, while the other one-quarter believed that the role should be filled with more than one person (using a team approach).

- Will your DPO role be filled internally, hired externally, or outsourced? About three-fifths of the respondents believed that the DPO role would be fill internally, with the other two-fifths of the organizations would be looking externally for their DPO, more wanting to outsource the role to and some organizations seeking to hire an external candidate if they can find one in the limited pool of experienced DPOs.

1.1.2.2 Takeaways

This survey was targeted at organizations that have already become members of a privacy or DPO association, so their understanding of the GDPR's requirements is likely further developed than that of the average organization subject to the GDPR. Nearly half already have someone in DPO role. While not a statistically rigorous survey with a limited number of respondents, there may be some useful takeaways. One takeaway is that there seems to be a recognition that an additional skill set may be required of the existing DPOs who continue in this role under the GDPR, as well as for new DPOs. Not only the new specifics of GDPR but also some of the technical assessments will require an expanded skill set, as discussed in succeeding chapters.

A second takeaway provides some insight in how organizations are looking at dealing with what may be the most difficult criteria for the DPO role, ensuring the DPO's independence and avoidance of conflicts of interest. Various techniques of outsourcing, separation of duties, reporting chains, independent contractors, conflict rules, legal ethics obligations, lack of other duties, and professional and personal qualities were among solutions suggested, along with access to independent legal counsel for non-lawyer DPOs and an independent budget. This requirement may evolve the most over time, as organizations work to make the role truly independent of those responsible for designing, operating, and overseeing the data protection, privacy, and information security functions in the organization.

In a final set of takeaways, organizations seem to fully understand the requirement for the DPO's reporting structure to the highest levels of the organization and the need for a vastly experienced resource to fill the DPO role. It was a bit surprising that most of these organizations are viewing the DPO role as being filled by a single person instead of a team, but that could be merely a snapshot of who answered this survey (it did not ask the size of the organization). Organizations clearly have many ideas about the right type of professional ideally suited to fit the DPO role and seem to consider outsourcing a viable alternative for filling the DPO role if suitably qualified internal resources are not available.

1.2 The Skills and Professions Of a DPO

Once it has been determined that a DPO is either required or it is better for business reasons to voluntarily designate one, then it becomes a matter of determining which job skills the person or persons filling the role must have to succeed as a DPO. This is assisted by understanding those competencies required to acquire certification as a DPO. Related to that but a separate consideration is which profession is most closely aligned to these skills to fill the role. If a single person is not doing all the DPO tasks, then the controller or processor should decide the different professions that need to be involved in filling the role as part of a team. Common misunderstandings in staffing the DPO role are also analyzed.

1.2.1 DPO Skills

The GDPR has certain requirements for the DPO, and this reflects directly upon the skills needed by the DPO role, either as a single person or a team. These skills can be summarized into a listing usable by organizations' management and human resources to identify qualified DPO candidates.

1.2.1.1 GDPR's Requirements for DPOs

Risk/IT: Recital 77 and Articles 39(2) and 35(2) require DPOs to offer guidance on risk assessments, countermeasures, and data protection impact assessments. DPOs must have significant experience in privacy and security risk assessment and best practice mitigation, including significant hands-on experience in privacy assessments, privacy certifications/seals, and information security standards certifications.

These skills should be founded upon wide-ranging experience in IT programming, IT infrastructure, and IS audits. While compliance checklists may be helpful, the DPO position first and foremost requires an experienced professional. Because risks constantly evolve, DPOs must demonstrate awareness of changes to the threat landscape and fully comprehend how emerging technologies will alter these risks. Providing guidance is like the lawyer skill of giving advice, using client-relationship skills to ensure controllers continue to seek such advice even if not in agreement and at the earliest phase.

Legal Expertise/Independence: Recital 97 and Articles 37(1), 37(5), and 38(5) specify "a person with expert knowledge of data protection law and practices" to assist the controller or processor, to be "bound by secrecy or confidentiality," and "perform their duties and tasks in an independent manner." DPOs must know data protection law to a level of expertise based upon the type of processing carried out. This signifies that DPOs could be licensed lawyers knowledgeable of not only the GDPR and other relevant EU legislation (e.g., ePrivacy Directive or pending Regulation) but also privacy and related laws in all jurisdictions their organization does business or outsources operations. Confidentiality is second nature to the legal profession. DPOs must have experience acting in an independent manner, indicating a need for a mature professional with client relationship and audit experience to handle the delicate task of discovering gaps, encouraging gap mitigation, and ensuring compliance without taking an adversarial position.

Cultural/Global: DPOs will likely be dealing with controllers and processors from different countries and therefore business cultures. DPOs must have experience in dealing with different ways of thinking and doing business and have the flexibility to marshal these differences into a successful result. Think of the simplified example of an organization with a retail presence in Europe, contract manufacturers in China, IT outsourcers in India, and headquarters in the U.S. DPOs should be based in the EU as recommended by the WP29 but also globally focused.

Leadership/Broad Exposure: Article 38(2) requires "The controller and processor shall support the DPO … by providing resources necessary to carry out those tasks and access to personal data and processing operations, and to maintain his or her expert knowledge."

DPOs will need to have leadership and project management experience, to be able to request, marshal, and lead the resources need to carry out their roles. They also must be able to critically assess themselves for knowledge gaps and request training in those areas. DPOs should have broad business experience to know the industries of the data controller and processor well enough to understand how privacy should be implemented to integrate smoothly with the way each company designs and markets its products and services and earns its revenues.

Self-Starter/Board-Level: Article 38(3) requires "The controller and processor shall ensure that the DPO does not receive any instructions regarding the exercise of those tasks … The DPO shall directly report to the highest management level of the controller or the processor." DPOs should be self-starters, with the competence and skills to carry out the role without guidance and to know where to find necessary information. DPOs must also have board-level presence and be able to deal with experienced business people who will not know the intricacies of DPO functions. Licensed external auditors, such as certified public accountants (CPAs)/chartered accountants (CAs), who audit compliance with laws, standards, and practices, are independent of the auditee, and report to the board, would have this type of experience.

Common Touch/Teaching: Article 38(4) allows data subjects to contact the DPO "with regard to all issues related to processing of their personal data and to the exercise of their rights." DPOs must be able to speak in the language of the average citizen, not in technical or legal jargon, to handle requests and complaints from data subjects. A common touch is helpful to DPOs in their role to protect data subjects' rights. DPOs must also have skills in both legal training and awareness raising, to ensure all data subjects are aware of their rights and responsibilities and to help train others to assist data subjects on specific requests.

No-Conflicts/Credibility: Article 38(6) allows DPOs to fulfill other tasks if "any such tasks and duties do not result in a conflict of interests." DPOs who are members of the data controller's organization may be performing roles that conflict with their DPO role. For example, a DPO also overseeing information security has a conflict when their security risk assessments and treatments are evaluated under their DPO role. Controllers are required to ensure that their DPO is not conflicted. It is best if DPOs are full time in their role or the role outsourced to an independent external DPO to overcome the possibility of conflicts. Article 39(1) states that DPOs are required "to cooperate with the supervisory authority ... [and] act as the contact point for the supervisory authority on issues relating to processing." A prior relationship with the DPA is helpful or DPOs must be able to establish instant credibility with DPAs based upon their wide experience, knowledge, credentials, and relationship skills.

1.2.1.2 Summary of DPO's Required Job Skills

The following summarizes these requirements into DPO job skills.

- Significant experience in EU and global privacy laws, including drafting of privacy policies, technology provisions, and outsourcing agreements.
- Significant experience in IT operations and programming, including attainment of information security standards certifications and privacy seals/marks.
- Significant experience in information systems auditing, attestation audits, and the assessment and mitigation of risk.
- Demonstrated leadership skills achieving stated objectives involving a diverse set of stakeholders and managing varied projects.
- Demonstrated negotiation skills to interface successfully with DPAs.
- Demonstrated client relationship skills to continuously coordinate with controllers and processors while maintaining independence.
- Demonstrated communication skills to speak with a wide-ranging audience, from the board of directors to data subjects, from managers to IT staff and lawyers.
- Demonstrated self-starter with ability to gain required knowledge in dynamic environments.
- Demonstrated record of engaging with emerging laws and technologies.

- Experience in legal and technical training and in awareness raising.
- Experience in dealing successfully with different business cultures and industries.
- Professionally licensed or certified in law, information security, data protection/privacy, and auditing, including ethical requirements for competence, confidentiality, and continuing education.
- Current or former EU resident who is independent and free of any real or perceived conflicts.

This view was verified against publications from the Network of DPOs for EU Institutions[5] and the WP29.[6] The former specified at least seven years of relevant experience, including knowledge of the institution and its data protection practices. It also included the following personal and interpersonal skills: "Personal skills: integrity, initiative, organization, perseverance, discretion, ability to assert himself/herself in difficult circumstances, interest in data protection and motivation to be a DPO. Interpersonal skills: communication, negotiation, conflict resolution, ability to build working relationships." The latter extended DPO roles to the internet of things and other emerging technologies (see below). DPOs may also have to deal with more complicated issues that are not included in job descriptions.[7]

The decision lies with each organization to find these required DPO skills in either a single person or several people, to locate them internally or outsource the role, and to manage this function under the CPO or let it operate independently. It would be optimal to have as many skills as possible in a single individual, for obvious reasons of cost, communication, productivity, and responsibility. While, of course, a DPO may rely upon technical skills of others, they must be sufficiently capable in all these areas to provide an independent assessment. It is up to each organization to implement its own DPO role keeping in minds its obligations and how a DPO will facilitate the likelihood of full compliance with the GDPR.

---

5 EDPS, Professional Standards for Data Protection Officers of the EU institutions and bodies working under Regulation (EC) 45/2001 (Oct. 2010).
6 Art. 29 DP WP, Guidelines on Data Protection Officers ("DPOs"), r1 (Apr. 2017).
7 *See* Thomas J. Shaw, *Outsourcing your DPO: real-life scenarios* (in the Appendix).

1.2.1.3 DPO Certification

DPOs may be subject to certification in some member states. For example, the Spanish DPA Agencia Española de Protección de Datos (AEPD) has published guidelines for the certification of DPOs.[8] This certification requires at least five years of relevant professional experience (or some combination of lesser experience and training). The four-hour exam covers the areas of DP laws, including GDPR, the ePrivacy Directive, and WP29 guidelines, plus relevant Spanish laws, accountability, including risk management and DPIAs (see Chapter 4), privacy by design (see Chapter 5), and compliance techniques, including InfoSec (see Chapter 5), DP audits (see Chapter 3), and emerging technologies (see companion book[9]). Certified DPOs must adhere to a code of ethics and take continuing professional training to use the AEPD-DPO mark.

The stated competencies of advising and supervising tasks for certified DPOs include the following:

- Compliance with principles relating to processing, such as purpose limitation, data minimisation or accuracy.
- Identifying the legal basis for data processing.
- Assessment of the compatibility of purposes other than those which gave rise to initial data collection.
- Determining whether any sectoral regulation may determine specific data processing conditions that are different from those established by general data protection regulations.
- Designing and implementing measures to provide information to data subjects.
- Establishing mechanisms to receive and manage requests to exercise rights of the data subjects.
- Assessing requests to exercise rights of the data subjects.
- Hiring data processors, including the content of the contracts or legal documents that regulate the controller — processor relationship.

---

8 AEPC, Esquema de certificación de Delegados de Protección de Datos, r1.1 (Oct. 2017).

9 See Thomas J. Shaw, *Emerging Technologies Law — Global Practice*.

- Identifying international data transfer instruments that are suited to the needs and characteristics of the organisation and the reasons that justify the transfer.
- Design and implementation of data protection policies.
- Data protection audits.
- Establishing and managing a register of processing activities.
- Risk analysis of the processing operations carried out.
- Implementing data protection measures by design and by default that are suited to the risks and nature of the processing operations.
- Implementing security measures that are suited to the risks and nature of the processing operations.
- Establishing procedures to manage violations of data security, including assessing the risk to the rights and freedoms of the data subjects and procedures to notify supervisory authorities and the data subjects.
- Determining the need to carry out data protection impact assessments.
- Carrying out data protection impact assessments.
- Relations with supervisory authorities.
- Implementing training and awareness programmes for personnel on data protection.

1.2.2 DPO Professions

To determine which professions to look to fill the DPO role, it is best to start with the GDPR requirements for the DPO's skills, qualities, and tasks include:

- Risk assessments, countermeasures, and data protection impact assessments.
- Expert knowledge of data protection law and practices.
- Perform their duties and tasks in an independent manner.

- Not receive any instructions regarding the exercise of those tasks.
- Perform other tasks only if these do not result in a conflict of interests.
- Handle data subject requests.
- Marshal resources and lead people and projects.
- To maintain his or her expert knowledge.
- Bound by secrecy or confidentiality, notwithstanding that the DPO can contact the DPA directly on any matter.
- Directly report to the controller/processor's highest management level and/or provide an annual report of DPO activities.
- Cooperate with and act as the contact point for the supervisory authority.

1.2.2.1 Professions Matching DPO Job Skills

The two professions appear best suited to carry out are the role of DPO, their availability and costs notwithstanding, are experienced privacy and technology focused lawyers and Information systems (IS) auditors licensed as certified public accountants (CPAs) or chartered accountants (CAs). A privacy-and-technology-focused lawyer is a licensed professional with hands-on experience with IT programming and operations, IS auditing, and privacy certifications/seals and information security standards, in addition to experience with varied privacy and information security laws, policies, and provisions. IS auditors would have experience with various types of attestation audits, including privacy and security. Both should have the appropriate professional privacy and information security certifications.

Both types of professionals should be able to carry out the following aspects of the DPO role equally well: reporting directly to the highest management level of the controller/processor, exercising the tasks of the DPO without receiving instructions, working in an independent manner, and being sensitive to not creating any conflicts of interest. Licensure rules for the regulated professions of lawyer and public/chartered accountant both require continuing competence, maintaining integrity, avoiding conflicts of interests, taking sufficient continuing education to maintain his or her expert knowledge, and being bound by rules of professional secrecy and confidentiality. Although lawyers tend to have a broader code of ethics to comply with, lack of compliance with their respective ethical rules by those in either profession could lead to loss of their ability to practice publicly.

Both professions need to have significant negotiation skills, although given their typical roles, the lawyer will likely have deeper negotiation experience. Both should have knowledge of risk assessments, countermeasures (including those implemented in software by programmers and in IT infrastructure), and data protection impact statements, although auditors will likely have more in depth risk mitigation experience. Both may have understandings of privacy by design and default, but the auditor may have more in-depth knowledge through assessing control design. Both should be able to marshal and lead resources, teams, and projects and handle data subject requests without difficulty, handle internal and external relationships, communicate effectively with all parties, educate controller/processor personnel and data subjects, and raise data protection awareness.

What tips the balance between the two is the requirement to have expert knowledge of data protection law and practices, which is something to be expected from the lawyer but not from the auditor. This requirement is more complicated than it appears, as it involves not only the GDPR but other EU law, such as the ePrivacy Directive (or its successor) and relevant cases, but also likely, given the global interplay of organizations, the data protection and relevant other laws and cases of many jurisdictions and the necessary conflict of laws analyses to determine which laws are controlling. In an independent role, a DPO providing legal advice and analysis who is not a licensed lawyer may also become involved in the unauthorized practice of law. If they instead use the organization's corporate counsel to perform the legal analyses, the DPO may no longer be viewed as independent.

Other reasons it is beneficial to have a lawyer in the DPO role include the advantages of legal privilege, competency and ethical mandates, being able to work easily with corporate and external counsel in the event of enforcement proceedings, and avoiding the unauthorized practice of law. If the DPO is not a lawyer, this means that they are going to be leaning heavily on the corporate counsel but when doing so, are they still sufficiently independent? Without the DPO's ability to rely on their own legal, IT, audit, and risk evaluations and not merely accepting those from internal staff, it seems that it would be difficult to maintain the necessary independence and avoid all potential conflicts of interest. That is why, for example, internal accountants prepare financial statements and licensed external accountants audit and opine on those statements, based upon their own independent professional judgment. And so should the DPO.

Therefore, the best professional to fill the role of DPO under the GDPR would be an experienced privacy-and-technology-focused lawyer. The privacy and technology focus of this lawyer is essential, as these would not be typical skills of the average lawyer. There are other qualities of a lawyer that also weigh in their favor as the best profession to fill the DPO role, including the use of legal privilege in certain cases when the controller or processor is subject to litigation or other adverse actions and possibly in their role as a witness or expert in legal cases. One area a DPO lawyer must avoid is acting as counsel for a controller or processor on data protection matters. The second choice professional to fill the DPO role should be an experienced and licensed (CPA/CA) IS auditor, one who has significant experience in leading various types of audit engagements. For either choice, the DPO team should have a member that complements the DPO, such as an experienced IS auditor when a privacy-and-technology-focused lawyer is the DPO.

Beyond those two professions, it gets more complicated for organizations trying to fill the DPO role with other types of professionals, with multiple people, and/or with a combination of internal, hired, and outsourced resources. As a rule, in these types of situations, organizations must stick hard and fast to the following two rules. First, they must not utilize anyone in the DPO role who could create a conflict of interest. For example, as a recent case in Germany[10] demonstrated, the role of IT manager is inappropriate for the role of DPO under current German law, given the required independence of the DPO from IT operations. Second, any resource filling the DPO role must have sufficient legal and technical skills to carry out an independent assessment of the organization's data protection practices without relying primarily upon the judgment of the organization's staff.

10 Bayerisches Landesamt für Datenschutzaufsicht, Datenschutzbeauftragter darf keinen Interessenkonflikten unterliegen (Oct. 2016).

1.2.2.2 DPO Hiring Errors

DPO jobs posted in the EU show some organizations are still learning about the requirements for DPO positions under the GDPR. The most common errors are looking for DPOs with too little experience (a few years is a common requirement), insufficiently broad job experience (focusing on only one of several needed disciplines), and lack of independence, with DPOs reporting into IT, legal, or compliance organizations instead of the board of directors as the GDPR requires.

Another error is that organizations assume that their current DPO or similar should be their DPO under the GDPR. That may certainly be valid, but it would be a useful exercise to vet the existing DPO against the job skills discussed above. When discussing the role of the DPO under the GDPR, examples are often cited based upon current experiences under existing legislation, primarily national enactments of the Data Protection Directive. While instructive and possibly the best historical examples that there are in the region, the DPO role under the new GDPR legislation is a somewhat different role, one that may require consideration of what is now required and intended before organizations that already have a DPO automatically slot that person into the DPO role under the new law.

Another common misconception, which many vendors are perpetuating, is that you can create a DPO merely with training and certifications without basing it first upon a broad foundation of existing diverse skills gained through years of experience. There is some belief that one can make a DPO out of an inexperienced resource. That is not accurate. What can be accomplished is for an organization to train an existing experienced resource, with many of the professional skills and responsibilities discussed above, in the specifics of the GDPR and hopefully deploy that resource in time into the role of DPO. While using an inexperienced resource can be viewed as the way forward for cost or resource-constrained organizations, they may be making a choice between full compliance with the GDPR and their other business objectives. Given the significant penalty regime of the GDPR, organizations should consider the need to staff the DPO role appropriately from the start to achieve their short- and long-term goals.

One other problem involves the fundamental flaw of confusing the role of the chief privacy officer (CPO) with that of DPO under the

GDPR. The role of a CPO could be described as someone responsible for complying with GDPR from inside the organization, setting policies and procedures to do so. But the new role of DPO is different. The DPO as specified by the GDPR must maintain independence and avoid conflicts of interest, in addition to acting as the point of contract, cooperation, and consultation with the DPAs. As the WP29 stated, "the DPO's primary concern should be enabling compliance with the GDPR." It then stated that "chief privacy officers ('CPO's) or other privacy professionals already in place today in some companies, who may not always meet the GDPR criteria, for instance, in terms of available resources or guarantees for independence, and therefore, cannot be considered and referred to as DPOs."[11]

While it is not essential that the DPO must be a lawyer, such a profession helps to address a problem raised by the GDPR. The DPO is required by the GDPR to have "expert knowledge of data protection law." The WP29 stated that DPOs "must not be instructed to take a certain view of an issue related to data protection law, for example, a particular interpretation of the law."[12] The DPO then will be independently providing legal advice on data protection law to the controller or processor as part of their specified tasks.

If the DPO is not a lawyer, then this could involve them in the unauthorized practice of law. Although a complex area of law not easily summarized, it appears that a majority of EU member states and a significant number of non-EU states including importantly the U.S. consider the provision of legal advice for compensation to be a "reserved" activity that can legally only be done by licensed legal practitioners. Those in certain jurisdictions like England or Ireland with a more limited number of legal activities reserved only for licensed lawyers may not understand these legal restrictions of other member states and non-EU countries.

Another likely issue that must be borne in mind is considering a simplistic legal compliance situation, not the more complex situations when the required expertise in data protection law includes the need to understand, coalesce, and possibly apply conflict of law rules to a large list of differing laws, regulations, and legal cases from different

---

11 Art. 29 DP WP, Guidelines on Data Protection Officers ("DPOs"), r1 (Apr. 2017).
12 Id.

countries, including the privacy and information security laws, consumer protection laws, labor laws, etcetera. Could this complicated legal work be done without a lawyer in the DPO team? Possibly, but if not, then independent legal counsel would need to be made available to the team.

In summary, privacy lawyers or licensed IS auditors would be the best professions to fill the role of DPO as specified under the GDPR. These are not the only professions who can fulfill the DPO role, just the best-qualified based on their skills and so should be the starting point for organizations search, within resource availability and financial constraints. If they are not designated as the DPO, these professions should at a minimum both be present as members within the DPO team, as their skills are a large part of what is needed to successfully fulfil the DPO tasks. Organizations will have to consider how to ensure these skills are available to support the DPO role regardless of who fills it. This would allow other types of professionals to fill the role of DPO, knowing they have support from the skill sets of lawyers and auditors who can perform their roles with the necessary independence to be able to assess the organization's compliance with GDPR.

CHAPTER 2

Initiating the DPO Role

Once the need for a DPO is determined, either as mandated by law or voluntarily undertaken by the organization, and the skill set and profession clarified, the role must be defined and then filled. This includes deciding whether the role will be staffed by an employee or outsourced to an external firm, whether it requires a part-time or full-time person, whether it will be worked by a single person or a team, the scope of the role, and the resources needed to support. The role must be announced both within the organization and to those outside the organization, including as mandated to DPAs and data subjects.

Once they become available, the DPO needs to undertake a series of initial activities to build a foundation with which to evaluate the organization for GDPR compliance. This involves a series of interviews with key stakeholders including upper management, data and process owners, and specialists who provide both the high-level perspective of how the organization deals with data protection and the more detailed view of the significant data protection issues that exist now or may soon. After having these initial discussions, a series of document reviews are required, with the two most significant being the data protection policy and the data and processing inventory.

DPO Areas of Focus

- DPO role definition and resources
- Insourcing or outsourcing the DPO role
- Startup interviews and reviews
- DP policy and data and processing inventory

2.1 Defining the Role and Outsourcing

The role of the DPO is defined by determining the scope of the position. There are many considerations in determining that scope, including the tasks to perform, whether it is part or full time, whether a single person or a team will fill it, the organizational scope, including whether the DPO is working for a single organization or multiple organizations jointly, where the DPO is to be located, the reporting lines of the DPO, and whether to insource or outsource the role. The resources needed by the DPO must be defined, budgeted, sourced, and made available. The outsourcing decision has many unique considerations, including what controllers or processors need to know before starting the outsourcing consideration, the questions they must ask potential outsourcers, and the contractual considerations.

2.1.1 Defining the Role

2.1.1.1 Scope

The DPO role must be defined in terms of scope across many different considerations. Under Article 39, there is a specified list of very high-level risk-based tasks for the DPO, including providing information and advice about the GDPR, monitoring compliance with relevant data protection statutes, including the GDPR and with the organization's policies, DP training and awareness raising, and communicating and cooperating with DPAs and data subjects. The specifics of these tasks can be used to build a position description for the purposes of advertising the role to potential candidates internally or externally.

Often the role description will include other tasks that are either implicit in the regulation or not strictly required by the regulation but may be a natural extension of the role. Examples of the former include regular reporting on compliance and risk to the organization's board of directors, working with other compliance groups in the organization in related disciplines or other geographies, and developing networks within the data protection community. Examples of the latter include keeping records of processing of personal data, taking the lead in developing data protection and related policy and procedures instead of merely advising, being a bridge between related disciplines, such as data protection, IT, audit, compliance, legal, and security, analyzing how the results of data protection related legal cases may impact the organization, and determining compliance with other relevant countries' privacy laws leading to synthesized global best practices.

A second consideration is whether the DPO position is a full- or part-time role. It can be part time, as the DPO is allowed to have other non-DPO tasks. Because the controller is required to ensure that there are no conflicts of interest for the DPO, any non-DPO tasks must not raise such a conflict. A DPO having the ability to determine the purposes and means of processing that defines the controller role would be such a conflict. The WP29 has identified the following roles as being conflicting: "chief executive, chief operating, chief financial, chief medical officer, head of marketing department, head of Human Resources or head of IT departments."[1]

As will be explained, except in the largest or most dynamic organizations or those processing sensitive data or other high-risk processing, the most important part of the DPO's role will what they do in their initial set of activities in discovering about and assessing the organization's DP practices. This may mean that the DPO is required full time in the first one, three, or six months, to assess and provide a compliance remediation roadmap but can drop to part time thereafter while performing compliance audits and training and providing advice on DPIAs evaluating new processing.

A third consideration is whether the DPO role is filled by a single person or the role is split up among several people. This decision would depend on the type of skill sets available to an organization and whether those are contained within a single person who is available to take on the role. If the required skills cannot be found in a single person but must be spread across multiple people, the requirements for independence and avoiding conflicts of interest must be closely examined and documented. In any case, the specific roles of each participant must be documented so that tasks do not slip through the cracks between the different individuals and one person in the DPO team should always be designated to have the final vote on all DP issues and that person should carry the designation of DPO.

A fourth consideration is the organizational scope of the role. According to the GDPR, a DPO is responsible for being involved with

---

[1] Art. 29 DP WP, Guidelines on Data Protection Officers ("DPOs"), r1 (Apr. 2017).

all data processing activities and issues for a controller or processor, but what exactly is the scope of those activities? Every business unit and every location of an organization is likely to be involved in the processing of personal data, but how closely does the DPO have to be involved with each business unit and location to understand what the DP issues might be? To some extent, this will depend to the extent that the data and processing is standardized across every business unit and location.

A DPO may also fill the role for multiple organizations under Article 37 such as a group of undertakings or multiple public authorities or bodies. A key issue when taking on the role for group of organizations beyond a similarity of organizational purpose and operating models would be easy accessibility of the DPO to all organizations to monitor compliance and carry out other tasks, including communicating with data subjects and DPAs.

A fifth consideration is where the DPO will be based. The WP29 has recommended that they be based within the EU for accessibility reasons. This is fine for EU-based organizations but may be less so for those organizations whose main establishment or only establishment is outside the EU. So, while an EU-based DPO would have better accessibility to EU data subjects and DPAs and speak their language, they may have less accessibility to the data protection evidence, IT systems, and organizational specialists if they are not co-located with the main teams of the controller or processor. This is further discussed in Chapter 6.

A sixth consideration is the reporting line of the DPO. The GDPR requires the DPO report to the highest levels of organization, "directly report to the highest management level of the controller or the processor." What this means exactly can be interpreted as the DPO should not report into an operational business or support unit but only to the board of directors. While ideal, this may not always work, given that not all DPOs will be board ready and would function better reporting in to the highest levels of operational management. Where they report clearly must avoid conflicts of interest that reporting in to any operational unit could raise. If not reporting organizationally, then the DPO should be filing status reports directly to the board.

A seventh consideration is whether to staff the role with an internal resource, hire a candidate, or outsource the position. The internal resourcing or hiring of a candidate would be based on the skills described previously in Chapter 1 and finalizing consideration of whether the role is full or part time, one individual or a team, its base location, and representing one organization or many. The question of whether those skills are best staffed inside the organization or outsourced is discussed in the next section.

To summarize, the considerations for defining the scope of the DPO's role are:

- Totality of tasks assigned to the DPO.
- Whether the role is part or full time.
- Single person or multiple people handling the role.
- Number of organizations supported by the DPO.
- DPO's primary physical location.
- DPO's reporting line.
- Insourced or outsourced DPO.

2.1.1.2 Resources

Whether the DPO role is conceived of as one person or as several people performing the role as a team, more than likely, there will be a need to access expertise that is not part of the DPO individual or team. That expertise must be allocated for in the budget and staffing plans if not generally available. Also, the DPO must maintain their skill levels, and so a certain amount of training courses or materials should be made available. In addition to themselves, the DPO is required to train and raise awareness in the controller or processor organizations, so they will need whatever resources are necessary to provide these functions.

In addition, the DPO will need various types of resources. Beyond obvious office space and equipment, this would include connectivity to appropriate IT systems and access to the necessary documents and communication methodologies. If DP issues are discussed on a company messaging system or web forum, the DPO must be added to these distribution lists. DPOs must be invited to all relevant meetings where DP issues are discussed, so need to be added to those calendaring systems. This includes not only management meetings but also technical meetings so that DPOs are involved early in new systems design. Sign-off checklists for new systems and technologies should include a step for DPO involvement and concurrence.

DPOs will need to be confidentially contacted by data subjects and employees of controllers and processors, so private office space, secure online and offline file systems, and direct private phone lines are all required. When there is a disagreement with the controller or processor that is material, the DPO, if they are not themselves a lawyer, may need access to independent legal counsel and could need an audit specialist to help with accessing compliance evidence. In any such case, the disagreement should be documented and submitted to the highest levels of management.

Finally, the DPO needs to be announced. Internally, this means making it clear the tasks of the DPO, their reporting line, their need for independence, and the expectation that they will be involved in all DP issues and activities. Externally this means providing contact information to data subjects, through online or app data protection policies (the name does not need to be provided). It also means providing the name and contact details to the relevant DPAs and contact details to data subjects, including employees. It is important, as the WP29 has pointed out, that professionals involved in data protection but not carrying the DPO designation and responsibilities not utilize the title of DPO internally or externally.

2.1.2 Outsourcing

2.1.2.1 Making the Decision

As the implementation of the GDPR nears and passes, many if not most companies outside those early starters have not yet filled their DPO role. With the limited quantities of qualified and experienced DPOs insufficient to meet the market demand, there will be a hurried rush to reserve any available resources for dedicated use. For everyone else, they will most likely need to outsource their DPO role, as allowed by the GDPR using a services contract.

There are several types of vendors ready to meet these needs. Roughly this breaks down into three categories. There are firms offering DPO cloud apps, task checklists, and work aids in varied formats. A second category are those firms offering DPO training and all manners of DPO skill certification. The third category comprises those firms that are offering real people to provide the DPO service, either full or part time, on monthly or hourly rates.

As the first two categories apply to companies that already have a resource designated to fill the DPO role, this section will focus on outsourcing of the role with an external resource providing DPO functions under a services contract. It will start by discussing what controllers or processors need to know before looking at outsourcing options, the questions to ask a potential DPO before selecting a certain candidate, then the various contracting issues to negotiate with a DPO outsourcing firm.

2.1.2.1.a Things to Know

Some controllers may be surprised by this, but hiring a DPO does not let them off the hook. Not one bit. The controller remains fully responsible for complying with the GDPR, including conforming to the principles for lawful processing of personal data in the GDPR, ensuring the rights of data subjects, protecting data through technical and organizational security measures, keeping records of processing, cooperating and consulting with supervisory authorities, providing notification of data breaches, carrying out data protection impact assessments (DPIAs) as appropriate, and ensuring the appropriate authority exists to transfer personal data outside the EEA.

Controllers who determine "the purposes and means of the processing of personal data" and processors working on their behalf should think of the DPO as someone who helps facilitate compliance for the controller's role, not someone who replaces it. The role of the DPO is to carry out the following tasks: Be timely involved with all issues relating to the protection of personal data, consult with controllers on DPIAs, instruct controllers and processors on their obligations under the GDPR, receive communications from data subjects regarding their rights and processing of their data, monitor compliance with the GDPR and related laws and the controller's policies, facilitate or carry out audits, attend DP meetings, and cooperate and consult with supervisory authorities.

Controllers also need to understand that DPOs must remain independent. DPOs have concurrent responsibilities to the controller's operational teams, to the board of directors, to data subjects, and to the local DPA and so cannot significantly tilt in any of these directions. Think of the DPO's independence as a center tent pole holding up the whole canvas and what happens if it leans in any direction. Controllers also must not instruct DPOs in the performance of their tasks and need to provide the DPO the necessary resources to carry out their tasks. Enhancing their independence is the prohibition that DPOs cannot be penalized or dismissed by controllers or processors for performing their tasks, including termination of DPOs working under a services contract.

Controllers must understand that they remain legally liable to data subjects for the processing of their personal data. While outsourcing is typically a risk treatment technique that allows for the sharing of risk with the outsourcing firm, that is not really the case in the outsourcing of the DPO role. Data subjects can initiate litigation against controllers and processors under the GDPR for damages resulting from infringements of that regulation, but there is no specification for data subjects bringing a claim against a DPO.

Controllers not established in the EU need to evaluate whether they require a DPO, as the GDPR applies to non-EU controllers and processors who offer goods and services to EU residents or monitor EU residents' behavior. All controllers, as a threshold question, must first know if a DPO is required. DPOs are required for public entities and for private entities whose core activities include processing that "require regular and systematic monitoring of data subjects on a large scale" or "processing on a large scale of special categories of data," plus processing of personal data on criminal offenses and convictions.

If the controller does not have the internal ability to analyze this question, perhaps it can be done and documented by tasking potential DPOs to justify the need for their role. Voluntarily designating a DPO even if one is not strictly required is encouraged by the EU's data protection authorities, who view DPOs as "cornerstones of accountability" facilitating GDPR compliance and a potential competitive advantage in business.

2.1.2.1.b Questions to Ask

Controllers outsourcing the DPO role must gain assurance through interviews, presentations, and questionnaires that the potential outsourced DPO has the professional skills and capabilities for the role. Some skills, such as the ability to communicate well and handle the required relationships, can be evaluated while interviewing a DPO candidate. A non-exhaustive list of questions to ask a DPO candidate should include at least the following, where "you" refers to the DPO candidate and not the DPO outsourcing firm:

- How many years have you been involved with the laws of privacy, data protection, and information security?
- How many years have you been involved with each of: IS auditing, IT infrastructure, data management, risk management, and software programming?
- What relevant professional licenses and certifications do you possess?
- What professional associations related to data protection are you a member of?
- What risk assessment methodology would you utilize as a DPO, and why?
- What types of DPIAs, privacy seals, and information security standards certifications have you been involved in?
- What types of organizations and projects have you led?
- Which countries have you practiced professionally in?
- Will you be resident in an EU member state for the duration of the contract?
- How do you stay informed on emerging trends in technology and law?
- How will you maintain your independence while working closely with us?
- Do you or your firm have any existing or potential conflicts of interest in taking on this DPO role?
- To what extent will you need to rely on your firm's knowledge, experience, and capabilities to supplement your own?
- Are you able to provide legal advice on data protection, what is the scope of that advice, and where will you refer matters beyond that scope?

- What experience and ethical obligations do you have to maintain confidentiality?
- What subject areas have you taught professionally and raised awareness on?
- What relationship do you have with the local data supervisory authority?
- How familiar are you with our industry, technologies, and processes?
- How do you address your potential exposure to legal liability for this role?
- In what manner and how often will you keep the board informed of your activities?
- (For non-EU controllers) What experience do you have with our laws and culture?
- What type of resources will you need to assist you in your DPO role?
- If you provide this service on a periodic basis (e.g., certain hours per month), how will you be available if the need arises (e.g., data breach, new systems, new processing)?
- What are the first three things you would do in your role as our DPO?

2.1.2.2 Contracting

Once organizations have decided on outsourcing the DPO role and selected their DPO based on their skills for the role, an agreement must be reached on a services contract. This involves certain legal considerations important to both parties, including addressing DPO-specific issues that may arise, and determining the types of outsourced DPO services desired.

2.1.2.2.a DPO Contract Considerations

Each party to a DPO services contract will want specific provisions. For the DPO services firm, the key terms are those minimizing their legal liability exposure. A controller/processor is liable for damage caused if its processing activities infringe the GDPR or if a processor acts "outside or contrary to lawful instructions of the controller." Article 79 allows a data subject to bring a lawsuit against a controller or processor for noncompliance that infringe their rights. A DPO is excluded from direct liability to data subjects ("DPOs are not personally responsible in case on non-compliance with GDPR" —WP29) but that does not mean that a DPO could not be targeted for legal action from the controller, processor, or affected non-data subject third parties. And DPAs can issue significant fines for noncompliance, though it is unclear when they might do so against a DPO, who is required to cooperate, consult, and be a point of contact with the DPAs.

While an outsourced DPO cannot have their contract terminated "unfairly" by the controllers/processors for "performing their tasks," what if the DPO does not carry out their responsibilities or does so negligently? What if the DPO provides professional advice that is inaccurate, not based upon an independent stance, or based upon a conflict of interest? Not only does a DPO need to have professional liability insurance to address claims for negligence in their role, but they also require services contract language that requires that the controller/processor indemnify the DPO for any third-party legal actions and limits the DPO's legal liability exposure within their relationship with the controller/processor.

Other contractual provisions should echo the GDPR, such as acknowledging the DPO's independence and the process to use when there is a difference in opinion. The contract should represent there are no current conflicts of interest. The contract term should be of a specific duration and not tied to any outside events or actions. There need to be specified turnover activities upon termination, including allowing the DPO to retain certain documentation. The DPO's budget for legal advice and training to maintain their expert knowledge should be detailed. Confidentiality rules and reporting lines must be specified.

2.1.2.2.b DPO Contract Issues

When negotiating the DPO services agreement, unexpected issues can arise. For example, an outsourced DPO may be offered compensation paid partly in company stock. Can the DPO accept this form of remuneration without a conflict of interest arising between their role in providing independent advice and wishing for rapid share price growth? Is an outsourced DPO required to only accept compensation in the form of cash payments not tied to the prospects of the controller/processor? Even if this does not create an immediate conflict of interest, but a conflict arose sometime in the future, would the stock have to be divested at no gain? Unusual compensation would have to be clarified in the contract.

The independence of the outsourced DPO requires separate data and email storage for legally privileged materials and communications, as the controller will retain possession of the DPO's company storage upon contract termination. Imagine the DPO has collected personal data by being contacted directly by a data subject under Article 38(4). When that data subject later demands their rights to erasure under Article 17, does the outsourced DPO have a sufficient legal basis to continue processing the data subject's data by retaining it on their separate data storage? To avoid this, an outsourced DPO should try to minimize their need to store data subject personal data. This separate data store based upon data minimization and defined retention periods should be clarified in the agreement.

The issue of independence arises when a DPO needs legal advice. It is best if the DPO is a lawyer so they can handle all aspects of data protection legal issues. There are times though when the DPO may want to turn to another lawyer for legal advice, whether to receive a second opinion, insights into unsettled areas of law, or details of cases or statutes in other jurisdictions. Which lawyer can a DPO take legal advice from? Advice from the controller's in-house counsel would call into question the DPO's independence. The controller's external counsel may with certain safeguards be sufficiently freed of conflicts. However, DPOs should understand that many law firms have stayed out of the outsourced DPO services market due to potential conflicts of interest. When a DPO and the controller and their counsel differ significantly in their opinions, the DPO would need to engage a separate law firm and the contract needs to address this possibility.

2.1.2.2.c DPO Contract Services

The main commercial focus will be on the services provided by the outsourced DPO. The WP29 recommends the controller "outline ... in the DPO's contract ... the precise tasks of the DPO and their scope." Outsourced DPO services occur both when fully engaged and as a series of potential startup services. The structure of the DPO role is also important, as the outsourced DPO does not need to be the doer of all tasks. Instead, the DPO may be in a role where they are instructing or mentoring less experienced staff who will eventually take over the DPO role. The controller/processor must decide on the DPO role structure, the tasks outsourced, and the startup versus ongoing services.

There is always the question of whether a controller or processor need a DPO. Sometimes a DPO is clearly required, and other times clearly not required, but the most prevalent situation is likely to be where it is either not clear one is required or when it would just be better to voluntarily have one than not. The WP29 recommends that "unless it is obvious" that a DPO is not required, there should be an internal analysis documenting the factors that were considered and the conclusion that was reached. While this is the responsibility of the controller/processor based on their accountability, there is no reason while the outsourced DPO cannot document and supplement this analysis, adding their expertise on data protection law.

Before beginning the ongoing DPO role, there may be will a variety of startup activities. As required tasks, the DPO would have to gain an understanding of the organization's data protection posture, shown through its policies, procedures, actual practices, and the level of awareness and commitment across the organization. The DPO also needs to understand the significance of gaps to reach a minimally compliant data protection program. The outsourced DPO must also understand in detail whether the resources and time that will be available are sufficient to perform the role, as well as the necessary communication channels.

Optional activities may have immediate deadlines or not fit within the time constraints of the ongoing role. For example, the controller/processor may require a data processing workflow/inventory to determine what personal data is being processed, a DPIA may be required for new technologies or processes, a data protection compliance audit may be required to create a baseline to measure future progress against, an analysis of the implications of GDPR may be necessary for organizations not sufficiently prepared, and other activities such as advising on information security policy creation and privacy by design may be needed. These are discussed in the next section.

2.1.2.2.d DPO Contract Provisions

The following are a minimum set of provisions an outsourced DPO contract should have. It must be emphasized that no contract should be drafted without undergoing legal review, especially as it relates to provisions impacted by local laws. There will also be a set of legal provisions common to any contract that is not shown below.

- *Parties*: The controller's or processor's legal entity is one party, and the DPO firm or individual is the other party.
- *DPO's services*: At a minimum, this should list the Article 39 tasks and then should add any other duties carried out by the DPO within the DPO role.
- *Controller's responsibilities*: At a minimum, this should list the controller's/processor's obligations under Articles 37–38 and other obligations under local law.
- *Handling differences*: Outlines the procedure engaged if the DPO and the controller/processor do not agree upon an important issue related to GDPR compliance and whether external counsel must be provided for.
- *Compensation*: Whether a DPO is working on a fixed fee or hourly basis and how additional hours are handled/approved.
- *Limitation of liability*: The DPO should limit their potential liability to the controller or processor, perhaps to the amount of fees paid to the DPO for their services.
- *Indemnification*: The DPO should be protected against any legal actions against them initiated by third parties regarding the services, such as those impacted by a data breach.
- *Conflicts of interest*: There should be a clear statement that there are no known conflicts from the services and any future conflicts will be notified to the parties and addressed at that time.
- *Confidentiality*: That the DPO will comply with professional duties of confidentiality or secrecy.
- *Training*: How the DPO will maintain their competence in data protection and related areas.

- *Term*: It is important to set an appropriate duration for the agreement that allows the DPO sufficient time to assess and implement the necessary changes to bring about GDPR compliance. At the same time, DPO cannot be penalized for performing their roles competently and so a longer-term period would allow be better demonstrate the organization accepting the DPO advice and guidance and possibly rejecting it when there are differences of opinion without resorting to a termination of services. A term of at least a year would seem to be the minimum appropriate term.
- *Termination*: Which duties will continue upon termination of the contract and how personal data is returned/deleted.

2.2 First Tasks of the DPO

Now that there is a DPO role defined and a person designated to fill the role, they can begin to perform their tasks as defined by the GDPR and their job description. To be able to evaluate GDPR compliance (discussed in Chapter 3), assess risk and advise on data protection impacts assessments (discussed in Chapter 4), be involved with assessments of information security, anonymization, data breach response, and privacy by design (discussed in Chapter 5), and transfers of data outside the EEA (discussed in Chapter 6), there is a set of activities that will familiarize the DPO with the situation they are in before moving on to these more complex tasks.

2.2.1 Start-Up Tasks

2.2.1.1 Meeting Key Leaders

The first activity that any DPO should be involved after understanding their organization's business objectives is to gain knowledge of how data protection is prioritized in those objectives. This can only come from meeting with the CEO of the organization and querying how they view data protection and then how they walk the talk. With some organizations, data protection is merely a compliance activity to which they dedicate the minimum number of resources to ensure that they make it over the line and avoid any regulatory issues. Other organizations see data protection as something that is more than just compliance, as it enhances their service or product offerings and delights their customers, thereby helping them to win and retain customers. There is, of course, every philosophy between those two end points, and a DPO must know where an organization sits and why.

Sometimes this philosophy may be deeply rooted in the organization, and sometimes it merely reflects the current CEO. Whichever it is, understanding this lets the DPO know who much they can move the organization to start viewing data protection as a potential competitive advantage. Beyond philosophies are the actual implementation, how much money is the organization spending, and how many resources are being dedicated to deal with data protection? How many people are directly involved in this and have their personal performance objectives tied to data protection results? What percentage of the workforce is required to attend regular data protection training? Does any positive mention of data protection show up in annual financial statement reports? Is data protection on the agenda on meetings of senior management and part of their KPIs?

2.2.1.2 Reviewing Existing Documentation and Evidence

After meeting the leadership, the DPO should then gather and review the existing documentation. The most important documents are the data protection policy and the data and processing inventory, which are discussed in greater detail in the next section. Other documents of importance will describe the IT systems using personal data, network and IT infrastructure diagrams, business continuity plans, existing data protection safeguards implemented, a list of all geographic locations the business is established in and does business in, and the standard customer and vendor contracts, and their data protection provisions and language.

What the DPO would be looking for at this early stage whether all the primary and secondary documents exist and are current and complete. The lack of such documents or their age or state of completeness may tell the DPO much about what they may need to spend their early time working with the controller or processor organization on. There should also be an evidence trail of how the organization is demonstrating compliance with the GDPR. Its current rigor will show the DPO the ability of the organization to withstand a data protection compliance audit in the near term.

The DPO needs to be looking carefully for obvious red flags as they review documents and talk with personnel, such as newer technologies being deployed, organizational and key personnel changes, business expansion into new countries or into new product or service lines, any regulatory investigations or qualified audit reports, or the lack of data subject complaints or subject access request processes.

2.2.1.3 Meeting Data and Process Owners and Certain Specialists

DPOs next should meet with select groups of operational personnel. This varies greatly by each organization and industry, but at a minimum, the key data and process owners, compliance specialists, corporate legal counsel, human resources, sales, IT infrastructure, and programming should be interviewed. The DPO would be trying to determine their current understanding and use of data protection safeguards and how they categorize and protect the various types of personal data for which they are responsible plus any projects under development or implementation, the current legal and compliance landscape, recent information security incidents, and how data protection training is used as part of the hiring and firing process and for continuing employees and contractors.

There are three questions to ask each of these specialists and owners at an initial meeting. These are not the only important questions to ask but can start the ball rolling. More detailed sessions with each of these specialists and owners will need to be held as part of determining GDPR compliance and building a plan to address any gaps. The questions for each follow.

Data owners:

- How do you acquire personal data and about whom?
- What types of personal data are acquired?
- How long is this personal data retained?

Process owners:

- What type of processing do you do on personal data?
- Is this data all automated or partially manual?
- How do you notify data subjects before processing?

Compliance:

- How is DP compliance currently demonstrated?
- What types of evidence is gathered about processing, and how frequently are compliance audits done?
- How are data subject rights enforced, including receiving and replying to subject access requests?

Corporate counsel:

- What are the legal bases for personal data processing?
- What EU privacy laws besides GDPR apply here?
- What non-EU privacy laws apply here?

Human resources:

- What type of sensitive personal data do you control?
- What type of DP training do staff receive?
- How do you protect personal data for departing staff?

Sales and marketing:

- How do you use digital marketing (website, apps)?
- Do you use any behavioral advertising techniques?
- Do you solicit customers via email or text?

Software development:

- How do test your code from design to production?
- How you protect your code against hacking (OWASP)?
- How do you use privacy by design and default?

IT infrastructure:

- How are servers/network protected against breaches?
- Are you certified by an international security standard?
- Do you have a tested incident response and business continuity plans?

2.2.2 Data Protection Policy and Data and Processing Inventory

2.2.2.1 Data Protection Policy

The most important document to review initially is the data protection policy and/or statement. The real data protection philosophy of an organization is shown by the written commitments it can be held legally liable for not complying with. Many organizations will not have spent sufficient time creating their policies/statement, while others have made a deliberate decision to minimize their public commitments and still others have spent the time to try and provide true transparency to their practices and give their data subject customers sufficient information with which to decide to participate. DPO's compliance efforts will include assessing the actual organizational practice against the written DP policies.

Before looking at the document, the presentation of the policy is critical. It should be located on an easily accessible website in clear readable text and easily understood text. If it is in an app, it may be presented as several layers due to the small screen size. While it will seem somewhat legalistic, this can be minimized in certain sections most important to the average consumer. Any section targeting children must clearly be written to their level of understanding while linking them to required parental consent. The policy should be separate from any terms of use/service online or terms and conditions in an offline agreement.

There are several important sections of the policy that must be identified, whether or not they are clearly labeled. This first section may seem simple, but it important to state the purpose of the policy, which should show the organization's commitment to its customers' data protection interests, rights, and freedoms. Second is the scope of the policy, enumerating whether there are any related legal documents (e.g., terms of service) that must be read to fully understand all data protection protections, and if it encompasses all personal data of customers processed by the controller or processor.

The DP policy should have a statement of DP principles, which would include the seven principles in Article 5: lawfulness, fairness, and transparency; purpose limitation; data minimization; accuracy;

storage limitation; integrity and confidentiality; and accountability. It should also have an expansive declaration of data subject rights, which include the rights to be informed, of access, to rectification, to erasure (be forgotten), to restrict processing, to data portability, to object and be free from automated decision making. Organizations seem loath to clearly state these rights in full as some are qualified rights but, assuming a rigorous subject access request response process has been established, there is no good reason not to openly declare these rights.

Depending on the type and sensitivity of the personal data collected and processed, organizations should be willing to publish factual statements of their leading InfoSec practices. The uses and types of encryption, testing methodologies, international standards adhered to, authentication techniques, incident management practices, data destruction standards followed, and primary and backup data center locations would be confidence-building information to provide to customers. The important legal point is that these all must be the actual practices of the organization currently and on an ongoing basis, to avoid enforcement actions and litigation concerning deceptive practices.

Every best practices DP policy will have sections that describe the personal data that is collected, how the personal data is processed, how and to whom the personal data is disclosed, and how the data is deleted or can be by the user, plus address sensitive data and vulnerable users, such as children. The data collection section should identify the categories of information that are collected directly from the user, collected from other third parties, derived from the consumer's use of the organization's services, websites, and apps, and information that may have come from a consumer's use of the internet and devices and any payment services.

The uses of the information would not only be for the primary services provided but also typically those undertaken to enhance the services provided, for security and to facilitate an online session, and perhaps to serve advertising. There is typically a discussion of the types of cookies used and other unseen processing, to stay compliant with the ePrivacy Directive/Regulation. Disclosures would include any expected in the primary services provided, plus disclosures to third-party processors used by the controller to perform services, such as IT or HR, to related parties of the controller, and to any advertising or marketing firms.

The policies will also have sections about it how data subjects can find out if it changes, and whom to contact for questions in general. The policy will also provide the contact details of the DPO. The DPO does not need to be named in the policy and can be listed as anonymously as being available through a dedicated email address, such as dataprotectionofficer@mycompany.com, via postal mail, or at a dedicated confidential telephone hotline. Employees may also be given an office location to visit for an on-site DPO. Emphasizing confidentiality of these communications and that data subjects can contact the DPO about any DP issues and their DP rights is important.

To summarize, the key data protection policy sections include:

- Purpose of the policy.
- Scope of the policy.
- Data protection principles.
- Data subject rights.
- InfoSec practices.
- Personal data collected.
- Uses of personal data.
- Disclosures of personal data.
- Retention and deletion of personal data.
- Processing of sensitive data and data of vulnerable users.
- Processing unseen by the data subject, including tracking.
- Contact details, including the DPO.
- Changes to the DP policy.

2.2.2.2 Data and Processing Inventory

The other important set of documents to review initially is the data and processing inventory. Unlike the data protection policy, this is unlikely to consist of a single document that is easily and reviewed. Starting with the term itself, there is some confusion over what this means and then what is required under the GDPR. Deliberately, this is defined as the "data AND processing" inventory. There are two unique components to it: one is an inventory of the data; the second is an inventory of the processing upon the data. While these could be constructed separately, due to repeating some amount of the same tasks, it is best done as a unified effort.

Why create a data and processing inventory? It will greatly help with many of the compliance requirements under the GDPR. Under Article 30, there is a requirement to keep a record of processing activities. The required information as discussed in Chapter 3 includes the purposes of processing for categories of personal data about categories of data subjects. Having a list of data will facilitate the ability to respond to subject access requests under Articles 15 to 22. Having the data inventory will also help document the legal basis upon of how personal data is being processed, as required under Article 6. It will also be a place to document how personal data is being secured, as required under Article 32 and how long it is to be retained. So, having a data and processing inventory goes a very long way to providing the necessary basis for compliance with a large part of a controller's obligations under the GDPR.

Creating a data and processing inventory is a very labor-intensive process. There are a variety of automated software tools that will help facilitate this, but due to the massive amounts of data held by the typical organization, this is a very difficult problem to target any tool at and reasonably expect a fully formed answer set. Beyond just knowing where data is located, who owns it, and the appropriate labels that go with each field in each record in each database, consider the difficulty when moving beyond structured records in relational databases. Much of the volume of data held today is most likely to be in semi-structured and unstructured data collections, such as video streams, word processing documents, spreadsheets, emails, texts, graphics, images, and the like.

The other major problem with trying to create a data inventory is that even if an organization is lucky enough to capture all the data types held, it will quickly become out of date. Data collection and processing activities are just so massive modernly that even the most disciplined and highly funded data teams in organizations would struggle to keep any inventory current. Consider the number of emails and text that arrive daily and how many of those may be on personal devices a BYOD policy. The numbers are quite staggering and require some amount of triage to determine what to attack first.

To begin to tackle the data and processing inventory project, the DPO, working with the controller and processor teams, would look to identify several starting points and then move forward on each. One would be to identify and interview all known data owners. All organizationally held data should have someone who is responsible for each type of data collected. These people should be located in business units. If the organization has a records or data team, they should also be consulted as data custodians may be separate from the data owners. The digital marketing teams would know what information they gather ad use to reach new customers. The corporate counsel may have information on data types, as well, as they would need to know how to freeze such data for litigation purposes.

The IT organization should have database administrators who should have schemas of the databases of varying kinds. The team responsible for backups and business continuity should also have to know what data is retained and is needed to be restored. The software team should have lists of all software used by the organization and the process owner of each can be queried for the personal data they are aware of. The compliance team would have details of personal data including some applicable to compliance with non-GDPR privacy statutes (e.g., ePrivacy Directive/Regulation). And the administrator who currently answers data subject access requests would have more information about personal data sources.

From all these sources and others identified as the interview process progresses can be used to begin to put together a current data inventory. Not all this data will be personal data, and so some type of identification needs to be made of what data is not personal data, which is outside the scope of GDPR. Implementing a new process means that revised or new apps or systems must thoroughly document the personal data they are processing, which will help to keep the data inventory from becoming outdated.

While gathering the information about personal data, as the same time the team should be gaining an understanding of what processing is being performed on the personal data in question. Additional information to discover is the type of security used to protect the data (e.g., encryption), the retention periods for the data, who has access to it, who is it disclosed to, and the legal basis being used to process the data. If done correctly, a data and processing inventory will begin to emerge, one that builds a foundation upon which to address many of the controller's or processor's obligations. Many iterations will be required, but from this data and processing inventory, the DPO will understand in some depth the GDPR compliance situation of their organization and be able to begin formulating gap plans to remediate any noncompliance.

To summarize, a data and processing inventory should gather information on personal and other data collected and processed by an organization, including the following details:

- Type of data, and whether it is personal data (e.g., name, IP address, etcetera).
- Whether the data is part of a special category (e.g., health).
- Where the personal data stored is stored (all the locations, including backups or mirrors sites).
- Types of processing done on the personal data.
- Legal basis for processing the personal data.
- How the personal data was acquired.
- Country the personal data was collected in.
- Who has access to personal data.
- Who is personal data disclosed to.
- Security techniques protecting personal data (e.g., encryption, pseudonymization).
- Retention periods and final disposition actions.
- Language of the data (if not obvious).
- Any restrictions attached to processing of personal data.

CHAPTER 3

DPO Tasks — GDPR Compliance

The principal task and the primary reason for the DPO role's existence is to ensure GDPR compliance by the respective controller or processor. It is easy to feel comforted that the controller or processor is ultimately responsible for GDPR compliance, but as an independent assessor of this data protection compliance, the DPO must understand what rules must be complied with, what effective compliance looks like for each rule, and what techniques to undertake to perform a sufficient audit to determine compliance or noncompliance. The DPO's assessment of that compliance needs to be independently arrived at without conflicts of interest.

This chapter looks in some depth at the various obligations under the GDPR that controllers and processors must comply with, with the controller list of obligations being far more extensive. Based upon these DP obligations of controllers and processors, a checklist and related questions are presented that can be used at a very high level to give the DPO their first impression on where their organization complies with the GDPR and where it is does not. For those areas where there is a lack of compliance, a list of initial action items must be built to address the most obvious compliance gaps. How to undertake a full compliance audit and the use of certifications and codes of conduct are also discussed.

DPO Areas of Focus

- GDPR rules for controllers and processors
- High-level checklist and questions for initial assessment
- Internal and external compliance audits
- Certifications and codes of conduct

3.1 GDPR Compliance — Controllers and Processors

Data controllers have many types of responsibilities under the GDPR to data subjects whose personal data they process. This includes how they collect the personal data, how they later deal with this personal data across many types of processing, and how they provide for access to the personal data for data subjects. Under Article 24, controllers are required to implement technical and organizational measures, including a data protection policy to demonstrate compliance with the GDPR.

It is important to first define what is meant by a controller. A data controller can be an individual, a legal entity, a government authority or agency, or any organization. The important qualification is that they determine the purposes ("why") and means ("how") personal data is processed or is named or nominated by a law that determines the purposes and means. A controller can delegate the determination of the technical and organizational aspects of the means to a processor while retaining questions, like "which data shall be processed," "which third parties shall have access to this data," "when data shall data be deleted," etc.[1] A joint controller is when there are two or more controllers jointly determine the purposes and means of processing by means of agreement or law.

The following sections describe those areas of the GDPR that the controller and the processor must comply with. The first deals with these various duties a controller has for processing personal data of data subjects, the second addresses the data subject rights a controller

---

1 Art. 29 DP WP, Op. 1/2010 on the concepts of "controller" and "processor" (Feb. 2010).

is responsible for responding to upon being exercised, the third section discusses security and breach, the fourth covers other obligations, and the fifth describes other statutes a controller may be responsible for complying with. The sixth section discusses processor obligations under the GDPR, and the final section reviews controller-processor agreements. More complicated compliance areas, like InfoSec, DPIAs, data breach, privacy by design, anonymization, and transfers of data outside the EEA, are discussed in Chapters 4 through 6.

3.1.1 Data Processing Obligations

3.1.1.1 Principles of Processing

When a controller is to collect and use personal data of another, they are subject to the seven principles described in Article 5, as follows.

Principle 1: Article 5(1)(a) requires that all processing on personal data is:

- Done lawfully (see following section for a description of the six lawful bases).
- Fair.
- Transparent.

Recital 60 stats that "fair and transparent processing require that the data subject be informed of the existence of the processing operation and its purposes" plus further information based on the circumstances and context. The need for transparency arises when seeking informed consent, when data subjects are provided information under Articles 13 and 14, when data subjects are exercising their rights under Articles 15–22, and after data breaches under Article 34, or when there has been a change in the processing. Article 12 requires the information to be in a "concise, transparent, intelligible and easily accessible form, using clear and plain language."

Principle 2: Article 5(1)(b) addresses collection, which requires that the personal data be collected only for purposes which are:

- Specified (i.e., what type of processing is/is not included).
- Explicit (i.e., in clear and unambiguous language).

- Legitimate (i.e., broader than the legal bases for processing, also considers other areas of law including human rights, consumer protection, contract, employment, etc.).

The WP29 has stated[2] that purpose specification requires that a controller perform an internal assessment before collecting personal data, sufficiently documenting the purposes in sufficient detail so that GDPR compliance can be assessed and data protection safeguards applied. The GDPR also requires that the collected data is not further processed with a purpose that is incompatible with the original purposes of collection (unless for scientific, historical, or statistical purposes subject to certain safeguards).

The WP29 considers further processing to not be merely processing beyond the original purposes specified but any processing after the original collection. In something that changes how controllers would analyze further processing, the DPD/GDPR "does not specifically refer to processing for the 'originally specified purposes' and processing for 'purposes defined subsequently.' Rather, it differentiates between the very first processing operation, which is collection, and all other subsequent processing operations (including for instance the very first typical processing operation following collection—the storage of data) ... In other words: any processing following collection, whether for the purposes initially specified or for any additional purposes, must be considered 'further processing' and must thus meet the requirement of compatibility."[3]

The compatibility assessment that the controller must undertake contains at least the following factors, per Article 6(4):

- Any link between the purposes for which the personal data was collected and the purposes of the intended further processing.

- Context in which the personal data was collected, in particular the relationship between data subjects and the controller.

- Nature of the personal data, in particular whether special categories of personal data are processed.

- Possible consequences of the intended further processing for data subjects.

---

2 Art. 29. DP WP, Op. 3/2013 on purpose limitation (Apr. 2013).
3 *Id.*

- Existence of appropriate safeguards (e.g., encryption or pseudonymisation).

Principle 3: Article 5(1)(c) supports the minimization of data by requiring that personal data processed is:

- Adequate.
- Relevant.
- Limited to what is necessary in relation to the purposes.

Principle 4: Article 5(1)(d) requires that the personal data be:

- Accurate.
- Kept up to date.
- If inaccurate for the purposes of processing should be erased or rectified without delay.

Principle 5: Article 5(1)(e) specifies that the retention of personal data in a form allowing for the identification of the data subject should not be longer than necessary, unless for certain research, statistical, or public interest reasons and only then if applying safeguards, such as pseudonymization to the personal data.

Principle 6: Article 5(1)(f) requires appropriate security of the personal data to avoid unauthorized loss or disclosure (see Chapter 5).

Principle 7: Article 5(2) gives the controller the obligation to not only comply with these principles but to be able to demonstrate this compliance.

For the DPO assessing compliance with the GDPR, these seven data protection principles must be applied to all processing of personal data by the controller or processor. The DPO should look for comprehensive forms of evidence, such as DPIAs (see Chapter 4) and for individual forms of evidence, including the following:

- *Principle 1*: Documentation of the lawful basis for processing; notices to data subjects when data is collected and when consent is the legal basis to support fairness and transparency.
- *Principle 2*: Assessment of purpose specification; compatibility analysis for all further processing.

- *Principle 3*: Documentation of the need for each type of personal data processed.

- *Principle 4*: Processes used to keep data accurate; communications from data subjects seeking rectification.

- *Principle 5*: Data retention schedules; pseudonymization techniques (see Chapter 5).

- *Principle 6*: Security assessments and certifications (see Chapter 5).

- *Principle 7*: All documentation supporting fulfillment of the controller's obligations and exercises of data subject rights.

3.1.1.2 Legal Basis for Processing — The Other Five

To process data under the principles specified in Article 5, the controller must have a lawful basis. Article 6 lists six categories upon which a lawful basis can be derived for processing of the personal data of a data subject, including the consent of the data subject and when necessary to:

- Carry out a contract which the data subject is a party to.

- Fulfill a controller's legal obligation.

- Protect the data subject's vital interests (or those of another individual).

- Perform a task in the public interest or official capacity.

- Give effect to the legitimate interests of the controller or another when overriding the interest, rights, and freedoms of the data subject.

Each of these legal bases requires additional clarification and explanation.

A data subject may have entered an agreement for a contract that requires the use of their personal data to perform the contract, such as using their address to deliver a package purchased online or their name and bank account details to bill them for the purchase. This legal basis includes processing in preparation for a contract but only for requests initiated by the data subject, not the controller. Background or credit checks therefore cannot be covered by this legal basis.

It is important to examine the use of this legal basis closely, as the personal data that can be processed on this basis must be necessary to the execution or preparation for execution of the contract. Any personal data not necessary for performing the contract could not use this legal basis nor if the data subject is not a party of the contract. Just because processing in mentioned in a contract does not allow use of this legal basis unless the processing is necessary. Consent and this legal basis should not be conflated or swapped without notice, as explained below.

A controller may have a legal obligation that requires the processing of a data subject's personal data. The law must be either EU or member state law, not that of a jurisdiction outside the EU and cannot be a contractual obligation. It must also follow the data protection principles of necessity, proportionality, and purpose limitation. This legal basis can arise when a controller is required, for example, to retain certain personal data under a statute for an extended period subject to regulatory audit or for reporting to a government agency. This basis can only be used when such processing is mandated by this legal obligation, not under general regulatory guidance, and the data requiring processing is clearly spelled out and not left to the controller's discretion.

Personal data can also be processed legally when it is done in the vital interests of the data subject (or another). A vital interest would be a matter of life or death, physical injury, or significant health risk. If an unconscious person needs their blood type revealed so that they may be treated by the emergency services, this would certainly qualify as processing in the vital interest of the data subject. Again, the legal basis must be used only when it is necessary to process this personal data to protect these vital interests.

When personal data is processed in the public interest or in the exercise of an official capacity, this is sufficient legal basis. For example, if a patient is feared to be carrying a sufficiently contagious and deadly disease, someone disclosing their name to public health officials would seem to be necessary and in the public interest. Those health officials may have the official capacity to then disclose this name to local hospitals to be on alert for this patient, and again it would be necessary. This legal basis is limited to the public interest and the exercise of official capacity of the EU or a member state, not other jurisdictions.

A controller may have their own legitimate interests to protect by processing a data subject's personal data. For example, this would allow them to complete a transaction that improves their business. However, this basis cannot be used without first balancing the interest of the controller against the interests and rights and freedoms of the data subject and outweighing them. Again, the processing must be necessary to give legal effect to these interests of the controller.

The WP29 has provided an analysis of this balancing test,[4] which can be complex by assessing the interest of the controller, the impact on the interests and rights of the data subjects, an initial balancing, then additional safeguards the controller applies to reduce undue impact on the data subject. The controller's or third party's interest being pursued must be real and present, must be clearly articulated, and be lawful in the EU. It could represent fundamental rights, public interests, or legally or culturally accepted interests.

The impact on the interests or fundamental rights and freedoms of the data subject could be looked at via risk assessment techniques (see Chapter 4) and should consider both positive and negative impacts. What must be specifically considered is the nature of the data, the way data is processed, the reasonable expectations of the data subject for use and disclosure, and the relative status of the controller and data subject. The provisional balance should consider compliance by the controller with GDPR principles. Some of the additional safeguards include data minimization, functional separation of the data, anonymization, aggregation, increased transparency, right to opt out, and privacy by design/PET (see Chapter 5).

Further processing that is not based upon consent or processing under a law protecting national and public security or similar interests must undergo an analysis as specified in Article 6(4) to determine if the further processing is compatible with the purposes for which the data was originally collected.

3.1.1.3 Legal Basis for Processing — Consent

Consent is the initial basis for processing personal data and the most complex. Consent has several preconditions. Consent for the processing of personal data must be unambiguously and freely given by statement or clear affirmative action (e.g., multiple swipes on a mobile phone screen), it must be specific to the purposes of the processing, and it must be

---

4 Art. 29 DP WP, Op. 6/2014 on the notion of legitimate interests of the data controller under Article 7 of Directive 95/46/EC (Apr. 2014).

based on the data subject being adequately informed before giving the consent of the identity of the controller, the purposes of the processing, the data to be collected and used, the right to withdraw consent, and any overseas transfers. A controller must be able to demonstrate that consent has been obtained if that is the legal basis for processing. Consent must offer control to the data subject on whether to accept or decline the offered terms and not be disadvantaged by not consenting.

On the "freely given" pre-condition, the WP29[5] states that "if the data subject has no real choice, feels compelled to consent or will endure negative consequences if they do not consent, then consent will not be valid… consent will not be considered to be free if the data subject is unable to refuse or withdraw his or her consent without detriment. The notion of imbalance between the controller and the data subject is also taken into consideration by the GDPR… Consent will not be free in cases where there is any element of compulsion, pressure or inability to exercise free will." Imbalances typically occur when the controller is either a public authority or employer but can be addressed if true choice can be offered without possible disadvantage.

Consent must also be unbundled from other types of consent that are being obtained at the same time (e.g., general terms and conditions) and granular for each type of processing undertaken. A written form used to obtain consent must be use clear and plain language and must be easily accessible. Any consent given must be as easily withdrawn, at any time, and without detriment, and the data subject must be informed of the right to withdrawal before giving consent. Children must be at least 16 years of age to provide valid consent, unless a member state lowers the age. There are special considerations for children, including the uses of their data.[6]

Consent cannot also be merged with the legal basis of being necessary for processing for executing contract for which the data subject is a party. Requiring consent to processing of personal data unnecessary for the performance of the contract would not be freely given. Processing of personal data necessary for the performance of the contract would more likely fall under a different legal basis than consent. So, processing of personal data strictly not necessary for performance of a contract would have no valid legal basis, and controllers should not request such data.

---

5 Art. 29 DP WP, Guidelines on Consent under Regulation 2016/679 (Nov. 2017).
6 *See* Thomas J. Shaw, *Consent to Children's Data — Is It Legal?* (in the Appendix).

Regarding this conflation of legal bases, once consent is withdrawn, a controller is obligated to delete data processed on this basis and to erase other personal data being processed on the basis of a performance of a contract. The WP29 states, "In cases where the data subject withdraws his/her consent and the controller wishes to continue to process the personal data on another lawful basis, they cannot silently migrate from consent (which is withdrawn) to this other lawful basis. Furthermore, any change in the lawful basis for processing must be notified to a data subject in accordance with the information requirements in Articles 13 and 14 and under the general principle of transparency."[7]

Further, "the controller must have identified these purposes and their appropriate lawful bases in advance. The lawful basis cannot be modified in the course of processing. Hence, the controller cannot swap between lawful bases. For example, it is not allowed to retrospectively utilize the legitimate interest basis in order to justify processing, where problems have been encountered with the validity of consent. Therefore, under the GDPR, controllers that ask for a data subject's consent to the use of personal data shall in principle not be able to rely on the other lawful bases in Article 6 as a "back-up, either when they cannot demonstrate that GDPR-compliant consent has been given by a data subject or if valid consent is subsequently withdrawn."[8]

3.1.1.4 Legal Basis for Processing — Sensitive Data

Article 9 defines certain special categories of personal data to be that which reveals:

- Racial or ethnic origin.
- Political opinions.
- Religious or philosophical beliefs.
- Trade union membership.

Or the processing of the following types of data:

- Genetic data ("personal data relating to the inherited or acquired genetic characteristics of a natural person which give unique information about the physiology or the health of that natural person").

---

7 Art. 29 DP WP, Guidelines on Consent under Regulation 2016/679 (Nov. 2017).
8 Id.

- Biometric data ("personal data resulting from specific technical processing relating to the physical, physiological or behavioral characteristics of a natural person") for the purpose of uniquely identifying a natural person.
- Data concerning health ("personal data related to the physical or mental health of a natural person").
- Data concerning a natural person's sex life or sexual orientation.

These special categories of personal data require a legal basis for processing under Article 9(2). The principal legal basis requires the explicit consent of the data subject. Other important legal bases include legal obligations of the controller under employment or social security laws, protecting the vital interest of the data subject when they are physically incapable of consenting, and when establishing or defending legal claims. There is a variety of other specialized circumstances that provide a legal basis, including several dealing with the public interest and health and via EU or member state laws.

3.1.2 Data Subject Rights

Data subjects have many rights under the GDPR regarding their personal data. These include when their personal data is first collected, when their personal data is later accessed or corrected, and when their personal data is deleted or ported.

3.1.2.1 Collecting Personal Data

Before personal data is first collected from a data subject, they must be provided certain information, unless the data subject already has the information. Under Article 12, the "controller shall take appropriate measures to provide any information" under Articles 13 and 14. Per the WP29,[9] this most commonly takes the form of a privacy notice or data protection statement/policy, as there is a very high penetration of internet access in the EU.

Article 13 states that this information shall include:

- Contact details for the controller and its DPO.
- The purposes and legal bases of processing.

---

9 Art. 29 DP WP, Guidelines on transparency under Regulation 2016/679 (Nov. 2017).

- Recipients of the data.
- If the data will be transferred outside the EEA.
- How long the data will be stored.
- Certain data subject rights (explained below).
- Right to withdraw consent or complain to a DPA.
- Whether provision is a statutory or contractual requirement and the consequences of not doing so.
- Existence of any automated decision making.

If the data was not collected directly from data subject, Article 14 adds additional requirements, such as a description of the categories of personal data processed and the sources from which it was gathered. There are additional exceptions, such as when it is impossible, requires a disproportionate effort, is subject to EU law that provides appropriate safeguards, or involves professional secrecy. This information must be provided within one month of acquiring the personal data or when first it is disclosed to another recipient or when first communicating with the data subject. In either case, if further processing is to be done for a different purpose, then the information must again be provided to data subjects along with the compatibility analysis.

3.1.2.2 Accessing Personal Data

Data subjects also have many rights regarding access to their personal data. Under Article 15, this is the right to know whether personal data about them is being processed, and if it is, to receive information like that which was to be provided upon collection:

- Purposes of the processing.
- Categories of personal data being processed.
- Recipients to whom the data have or will be disclosed.
- Retention periods.
- Source of data not collected directly from data subject.
- Existence of automated decision making.

- Existence of data subject's rights to rectification, erasure, to object to or restrict processing, and complain to DPA.
- Safeguards for any data transferred outside the EEA or to an international organization.

The data subject has the right to receive a copy of the data free of charge and in electronic form if requested electronically. The controller must either provide this information (and all the following request types) within a month or provide within a month a reason why they cannot provide it timely (e.g., for complex or voluminous requests), in which case they can have up to two additional months to provide the information. This can have certain legal implications.[10]

3.1.2.3 Rectifying and Deleting Personal Data

Data subjects have rights to correct and erase their personal data and to stop its processing if not correct. Under Article 16, data subjects can require controllers to correct an inaccurate personal data and to complete any incomplete data by submitting the additional information. Data subjects also have the right under Article 17 to have their personal data erased, when the following grounds exist:

- Personal data is no longer necessary for the purposes of the processing for which it was collected.
- Consent is withdrawn, and there is no other legal basis to continue processing the personal data.
- Data subject successfully objects (discussed below).
- Personal data is unlawfully being processed
- Erasure is required under a legal obligation of the controller
- Personal data of children collected as part of information society services

The controller has an obligation if they have made this personal data public to notify other controllers that the data subject has requested erasure of any copies of or links to the personal data. There are several limitations on the right to erasure, including when contrary to the rights

---

10 See Thomas J. Shaw, *Subject access requests under the GDPR — Uses in litigation* (in the Appendix).

of freedom of expression and receiving information, in the public interest or for public health, for research of statistical purposes, when establishing or defending legal claims, or if complying with legal obligations.

3.1.2.4 Restricting and Objecting to Processing of Personal Data

In addition to erasure of personal data, data subjects have the rights to restrict processing of their personal data. Under Article 18, in the following cases, restriction of processing is possible:

- Accuracy of the personal data is contested.
- Processing is unlawful.
- Personal data is no longer required by the controller for the purposes of processing but needed by the data subject for the establishment or defense of legal claims.
- Data subject has objected to the processing (discussed below).

Personal data that has been so restricted cannot be processed in any manner except for storage without consent, unless one of the following applies:

- Establishment or defense of legal claims.
- Protect the rights of another.
- Important public interest.

Any restoration of previously restricted processing requires notice to the data subject. Rectification, erasure, and restriction of processing requires the controller to notify any recipient to whom the personal data was disclosed, unless the effort is disproportionate.

Data subjects may object at any time to the processing of their personal data under Article 21 when it is done on the legal bases of performing a task in the public interest or official capacity or when giving effect to the legitimate interests of the controller or another. The processing must stop unless the controller can demonstrate a "compelling legitimate grounds for the processing which override the interests, rights and freedoms of the data subject" or for the establishment or defense of legal claims. Processing of their personal data for direct marketing purposes, including profiling, can be objected to any time by the data subject.

Data subjects also have the right under Article 22 to not be subject to decisions based solely on automated processing, including profiling, which produces legal or similar significant effects on them. A human cannot have meaningful role in the automated decision. The exceptions are if the decision is related to the execution of a contract, is based on explicit consent, or is authorized by law and is not based on a special category of data without explicit consent. Data subjects must be informed of this type of processing, the logic used, and the consequences of the processing.

The GDPR defines profiling to be "any form of automated processing of personal data consisting of the use of personal data to evaluate certain personal aspects relating to a natural person." According to the WP29,[11] this allows individuals to be placed into a category or make predictions about their behavior, abilities, or interests. Profiling may or may not be involved with solely automated decision making, but profiling not involved with solely automated decision making is subject to the same obligations and data subject rights as any other processing.

3.1.2.5 Porting Personal Data

Data subjects now have the right to receive their personal data that they provided back in electronic format. Under Article 20, this data (and relevant metadata) is to be provided either directly to the data subject or to the successor controller, in a "structured, commonly used and machine-readable format." This assumes that the processing is automated and based on either consent or the execution of a contract to which the data subject is a party. The right to porting data can then be followed on by the right to erasure of the personal data, but it is not required, and the data would remain during the stated retention period.

The WP29 states that the right of portability providing direct transfers between controllers will enhance the free flow of data across the EU and increase competition.[12] The WP29 encourages controllers to develop automated tools and APIs to facilitate this right and interoperability standards for controller to controller transmissions. Further, the right applies to data provided by the data subject and any data generated by the data subject's use of a service or device but not any data inferred or

---

11 Art. 29 DP WP, Guidelines on Automated individual decision-making and Profiling for the purposes of Regulation 2016/679, r1 (Feb. 2018).
12 Art. 29 DP WP, Guidelines on the right to data portability, r1 (Apr. 2017).

derived from observing the data subject's activity. Portability does not affect data retention periods, such that controllers do not have to retain data just to satisfy future portability requests.

The controller receiving the ported personal data from the prior controller needs to verify that the data is necessary, relevant, and not excessive for purposes of the new processing and is not obligated to keep any data that is not. The receiving controller needs to provide the information required under Articles 13 and 14 to the data subject when receiving ported data. The rights and freedoms of others cannot be impacted by transferring data under the right of portability

3.1.2.6 Complaints and Judicial Remedies

Data subjects now have rights to initiate a complaint with the DPA under Article 79 in either their member state of habitual residence, work, or an infringement for processing of their personal data that violates the GDPR or to seek a judicial remedy under Article 81 against the controller in the member state of the controller's establishment or the data subject's habitual residence. The controller is responsible to data subjects under Article 82 for damage caused by processing infringing the GDPR. DPAs may also levy administrative fines against controllers under Article 83 of up to two percent and four percent of global revenues, depending on the article violated and many other considerations.

3.1.3 Security and Breach

Controllers also have obligations regarding the security of the personal data under their control and in the event of a breach of that personal data. How to evaluate these two areas require special technical knowledge, which is discussed in greater detail in Chapter 5. This section presents the legal obligations under the GDPR.

3.1.3.1 InfoSec Safeguards

The controller is required to implement organizational and technical controls considering the risk involved and regularly test and evaluate those controls. Risks include the unauthorized disclosure, loss, or alternation of personal data. Suggested controls include encryption, pseudonymization, and controller employees only processing personal data under instructions. The security measures implemented should consider the cost; the current state of the art in technology; the "nature, scope, context and purposes of processing"; and the risks to the rights and freedoms of the data subjects. The InfoSec program should focus on the aspects of confidentiality, integrity, and availability (and resilience) of the systems and services performing the processing of personal data. This also includes the ability to restore access to and availability of personal data after a security or other incident.

3.1.3.2 Data Breach Notification

When a personal data breach occurs, the controller is required to notify both the DPA and affected data subjects under certain circumstances. A personal data breach is defined as "breach of security leading to the accidental or unlawful destruction, loss, alteration, unauthorised disclosure of, or access to, personal data transmitted, stored or otherwise processed." Loss involves the loss of control, custody, or access to the data. Notification attempts to minimize damages, including "loss of control over their personal data, limitation of their rights, discrimination, identity theft or fraud, financial loss, unauthorised reversal of pseudonymisation, damage to reputation, and loss of confidentiality of personal data protected by professional secrecy."[13]

Under Article 33, the DPA must be notified within 72 hours of becoming aware of a breach that compromises personal data unless there is not likely to be risk to the rights and freedoms of data subjects. This may require an initial investigation to ascertain whether personal data has been compromised. The WP29 has stated "the ability to detect, address, and report a breach in a timely manner should be seen as essential elements"[14] of the security requirements under Article 32.

The WP29 recommends the evaluation of the risk to the rights and freedoms of data subjects include the following criteria:

- Type of breach.
- Nature, sensitivity, and volume of data.
- Ease of identification of individuals.
- Severity of consequences for individuals.

---

13 Art. 29 DP WP, Guidelines on Personal data breach notification under Regulation 2016/679, r1 (Feb. 2018).
14 Id.

- Special characteristics of the individuals.
- Number of affected individuals.
- Special characteristics of the data controller.

It is the risk assessed by severity of the potential impact on the rights and freedoms of individuals and the likelihood of these occurring that the controller must determine if mandating notification.

The following information must be provided to the DPA with the notification or in stages without undue delay:

- Nature of the breach, including categories (including vulnerable data subjects) and numbers of data subjects and personal data records.
- Likely consequences of the breach.
- Measures taken to deal with the breach.
- Contact details if more information is required.

When the data subjects in multiple EU member states are likely to be impacted, then the controller must notify at a minimum their lead supervisory authority,[15] likely the local DPA but can notify all applicable DPAs. When reported to a DPA or not, the controller needs to document every personal data breach, its causes and effects, the personal data impacted, and the actions taken by the controller, plus the reasons not to notify the DPA. Controllers may have existing obligations to report breaches under other EU laws, as well, such as providers of public electronic communications services.[16]

Affected data subjects must be notified by the controller without undue delay when the personal data breach is likely to lead to a "high risk to the rights and freedoms" of these data subjects. This is a higher threshold than the notification to DPAs, which is based on a risk instead of a high risk. Notification to data subjects must contain at least the nature of the breach, the likely consequences, the measures taken, and the contact details described above. Any steps data subjects can take to protect themselves should be included, as well.

---

15 *See* Art. 29 DP WP, Guidelines for identifying a controller or processor's lead supervisory authority, r1 (Apr. 2017).
16 *See* Thomas J. Shaw, *Information and Internet Law — Global Practice*, Ch. 4.

Notification to data subjects is not required when the personal data would be unintelligible to an unauthorized person, such as through the use of a highly reliable encryption algorithm and the encryption keys have not been compromised, if the high risk has been mitigated through subsequent actions of the controller or processor, or it would involve disproportionate effort and a public communication would suffice.

3.1.3.3 DPIAs/Prior Consultation

Under Articles 35 and 36, controllers are required to undertake data protection impact assessments (DPIAs) for certain high-risk processing, and if the measures taken by the controller may not sufficiently mitigate that risk, to consult with the DPA before engaging in this high-risk processing. The details of carrying out a DPIA requires certain procedural and technical knowledge and is therefore the subject of Chapter 4.

3.1.4 Other Obligations

3.1.4.1 Record Keeping

Controllers are required to keep written records of the processing of personal data and make them available to DPAs on request. Under Article 30, these records should contain the following information:

- Contact details of the controller and DPO.
- Purposes of processing.
- Categories of personal data and of the data subjects.
- Categories of recipients to whom data had or will be disclosed
- Transfers of personal data outside the EEA or to international organizations
- Data retention time periods
- General description of relevant InfoSec controls

Organizations are exempt from these record-keeping requirements if they employ less than 250 people, process personal data occasionally, do not process special categories of personal data, and there is not likely to be a risk to the rights and freedoms of data subjects.

3.1.4.2 DPAs

Under Article 31, controllers are required to cooperate with requests from DPAs carrying out their prescribed tasks. DPAs are authorized to obtain information from controllers, gain access to the personal data they process, and access to any controller facilities containing data processing equipment. Controllers can be warned or reprimanded by DPAs for noncompliant processing, ordered to comply with data subject requests exercising their rights or to bring their processing into compliance, ordered to stop data transfers outside the EEA or to an international organization, and can be fined for noncompliance.

3.1.4.3 DPOs

The controller's responsibilities for designating, resourcing, and tasking DPOs under Articles 37–39 were discussed in Chapters 1 and 2.

3.1.4.4 Transfers Outside the EEA

The controller's obligations for transfers of personal data outside the EEA under Articles 44–49 are quite involved and so are discussed in Chapter 6.

3.1.4.5 Employees

Article 88 allows member states to pass laws to protect the rights and freedoms of employees in the processing of their personal data. In particular, this focuses on new technologies' ability to monitor employees during recruitment, termination, performance of employment contracts, organization of work, equality and diversity, health and safety, employee property, and rights and benefits of employment. The WP29[17] described such scenarios to include monitoring social media use during recruitment or employment; monitoring IT and communications use at work or home; monitoring via wearables, company equipment, or company vehicles; and disclosure of personal data to third parties or overseas transfers. It reiterated that consent is unlikely to be valid legal basis in the employment context, due to the imbalance of power and potential adverse consequences for employees. The WP29 reminded employers that processing should be necessary, legal, fair to employees, transparent, and proportionate.

---

17 Art. 29 DP WP, Op. 2/2017 on data processing at work (June 2017).

3.1.4.6 Public Authorities

Governmental organizations and those performing public tasks have several areas where they are treated differently than private sector organizations. This includes for the legal basis to processing of personal data where the use of consent would be difficult due to the imbalance of power and the legitimate interest of the controller is not allowed as public authorities should find their legal basis for processing via statute. Under Article 86, public authorities must respond to laws requiring access to official documents while safeguarding DP rights. Public authorities are also required to appoint DPOs.

The European data protection supervisor (EDPS) is responsible for data protection in EU public bodies and has published various tools to help public authority DPOs, such as spreadsheet templates for registers and inventories of data processing operations, a list of the tasks, duties and powers of a public authority DPO, the professional standards for public authority DPOs,[18] and their role in facilitating compliance with the applicable data protection laws for EU institutions.[19]

3.1.5 Other Statutes

3.1.5.1 ePrivacy Directive (and potential Regulation)

The DPO is tasked not only with monitoring compliance with the GDPR, but also with "with other Union or Member State data protection provisions." The most obvious example of this would be the ePrivacy Directive, soon to be transformed into the ePrivacy Regulation (though just how soon is unknown at this writing). This may lay additional obligations upon a controller. The ePrivacy Directive[20] specifies that those organizations providing publicly available electronic communication services have certain obligations to the consumer of their services. This includes providing information to the subscriber if

---

18 EDPS, Professional Standards for Data Protection Officers of the EU institutions and bodies working under Regulation (EC) 45/2001 (Oct. 2010).
19 EDPS, Position paper on the role of Data Protection Officers in ensuring effective compliance with Regulation (EC) 45/2001 (Nov. 2005).
20 Directive 2002/58/EC of the European Parliament and of the Council of 12 July 2002 concerning the processing of personal data and the protection of privacy in the electronic communications sector (Directive on privacy and electronic communications), as modified by 2009/132/EC.

the provider will store or access information on their terminal equipment (e.g., computer or mobile phone) and giving the subscriber the right to refuse such processing. This permission extends to the placing of cookies on end-user devices.

The providers also have obligations to safeguard the personal and traffic data on their networks concerning subscribers and users. Traffic and location data must be deleted or anonymized when no longer required and location data requires the consent of the subscriber or user to process. Direct marketing emails and texts require the consent of the recipient (opt-in) unless they are an existing customer, who can opt-out. Senders can conceal their identity or not provide a valid opt-out address. There are data breach notification requirements based on the risks to the users.

3.1.5.2 Implementing Statutes

The GDPR is a regulation that applies to all member states, but it left numerous opportunities for member states to codify derogations and other restrictions. To understand what member states can do in the implementing statutes, the following discusses the Irish draft statute.[21] In its first substantive section, it creates the Data Protection Commission with multiple possible commissioners, whereas currently there is a single commissioner and later addresses DP audits, inspections, enforcement, and administrative fines. Certain offenses are criminal, such as unauthorized disclosures by processors, disclosure of personal data obtained without authority, and certain actions by corporate directors. It has also a section on data protection relating to law enforcement.

For the GDPR, it starts by setting the age of digital consent for children at 13 years of age. It then allows the government to require DPOs for certain classes of controllers or processors. It lists specific safeguards to protect the rights and freedoms of data subjects to include: explicit consent, processing limitations, strict erasure time limits, targeted training, logging, pseudonymization, encryption, and the designation of a DPO. The government retains the ability to restrict transfers of personal data outside the EEA as a matter of public policy. Further processing is allowed to prevent threats to national security or preventing criminal offenses. The processing of sensitive data is allowed for legal claims or defenses. There are numerous specifics for the

---

21 Ireland, Data Protection Bill (Jan. 2018).

processing of sensitive data, for public interest, freedom of expression, criminal convictions, statistics, and research, etcetera. Data subject rights are restricted when necessary for judicial independent, parliamentary privilege, and cabinet confidentiality; preventing crimes; administering taxation; exercise or defense of legal claims; enforcement of civil laws claims; or to estimate the liability of a controller for a claim. These data subject rights are also restricted when involving expressions of opinion given in confidence or for data provided to the DPC.

3.1.6 Processors under the GDPR

3.1.6.1 GDPR Requirements

Processors work under the direction of controllers and so inherit certain of the obligations of controllers. A processor can be either an individual or a private or public organization that "processes personal data on behalf of the controller." Importantly, any processor who determines the purposes and means of processing will be considered a controller with all the inherent obligations for that processing.

Under Article 28, processors can only be used by controllers if they provide guarantees that their organizational and technical safeguards are such that ensure compliance with the GDPR. A processor cannot engage a subprocessor without prior written authorization from the controller. Under Article 29, processors cannot process personal data unless they do so under instructions from the controller. Processors must notify controllers of any instructions that they believe are in violation of the GDPR.

In addition to DPA administrative fines, processors need to understand that penalties for not following the instructions of controllers may lead to criminal convictions. Article 84 gives member states the ability to set penalties especially for infringements not already subject to administrative fines under Article 83. For example, under the bill implementing the GDPR in Ireland, an employee or agent of a processor who knowingly or recklessly discloses personal data without doing so under instructions from a controller can be fined up to 50,000 euros or sentenced to imprisonment of up to five years.

3.1.6.2 Other Requirements

Some of the obligations that apply to the controller likewise apply to the processor. Under Article 30, a processor is also required to keep a record of processing carried out on behalf of a controller. This record should include the names and contact details of controllers and their DPOs and the processors involved, categories of processing carried out, any transfers outside the EEA or to international organizations, and a general description of the technical and organizational controls. Under Article 32, the processor has the same InfoSec requirements as the controller. The processor must notify the controller without undue delay under Article 33 for any personal data breach it becomes aware of.

Processors are generally required to deal with DPAs in the same manner as controllers and can be subject to judicial remedies brought by data subjects. Processors are liable for damage "only where it has not complied with obligations of this Regulation specifically directed to processors or where it has acted outside or contrary to lawful instructions of the controller." Those obligations include helping the controller to comply with the GDPR and providing information to demonstrate that compliance.

The CNIL has produced a guide for processors.[22] This instructs them on their obligations under the GDPR and suggests that they designate a DPO review existing contracts for GDPR compliance, ensuring they keep a record of processing. It also provides a template contract with five sections, including 15 obligations that is GDPR compliant. It summaries that a processor will be liable if they do not follow the instructions of controllers or outside the scope, help them comply or provide information for compliance or tell them of illegal instructions, use subprocessors without approval or proper safeguards, or don't keep records of processing or appoint a DPO when mandatory.

---

22 CNIL, Règlement européen sur la protection des données personnelles — Guide du sous-traitant (Sept. 2017).

3.1.7 Processor — Controller Agreement

3.1.7.1 GDPR

Under Article 28, there is a list of requirements for the processor-controller agreement. This leads off by mandating that the processor is bound to the agreement, which sets out the subject matter and duration of the processing, the nature and purposes of processing, the types of personal data, the categories of data subjects, and the obligations and rights of the controller. The agreement must be in writing and needs to specify that the processor:

- Processes the personal data only on "documented instructions from the controller."
- Transfers outside the EEA or to international organizations must either be under instruction from the controller or specified by law.
- Its employees who are authorized to process the data are under a commitment of confidentiality.
- Has implemented the InfoSec requirements listed above for controllers.
- Does not engage subprocessors without prior instruction from the controller, then the subprocessor must agree to the same obligations as specified in the controller-processor agreement.
- The original processor is liable to the controller regarding the subprocessor's performance of its obligations.
- Assists the controller to the extent possible with the controller's obligations to respond to data subject requests exercising the data protection rights.
- Assists the controller in complying with the controller's InfoSec, data breach notification, and DPIA/prior consultation obligations.
- Deletes or returns all personal data to the controller at the end of the agreement unless legal obligation.
- Makes available to the controller information necessary to demonstrate GDPR compliance.

- Allows and contributes to audits and inspections by the controller.

3.1.7.2 Other Provisions in the Agreement

Any agreement between a controller and processor would have provisions that at a minimum would deal with naming the parties involved, list their physical addresses and contact details, state the services offered and the prices for those services, list the service levels associated with those services, define who owns any intellectual property created and used and other IP protections related to trademark and copyright, address the limitations of liability for the processor in their role and what would cause that limitation to not be enforced, describe indemnity for the processor against any third-party litigation assuming the processor has followed the controller's instructions and has carried out their duties competently and with due care, require complying with all laws, state any restrictions on the right to audit (e.g., with certain notice, during certain hours, limits to frequency, reliance on reports of auditors, etcetera), and define when any of the terms and conditions might not apply.

ICO has published guidance on the controller-processor agreement[23] that includes a checklist of what should be in this contract. This has both compulsory terms and those that should be included as good practice, as well as a list of the direct responsibilities of the processor under the GDPR.

3.2 GDPR Compliance — Assessments, Audits, Certifications

There is a variety of times and techniques when and how compliance with the GDPR must be ascertained. Knowing that the controller or processor retains responsibility for compliance with the GDPR, the DPO is required to advise and monitor compliance with the GDPR. The DPO is going to perform an initial high-level assessment of compliance, as discussed in Chapter 2, using perhaps the checklist and questions presented below. Later, they will engage in more formal compliance

---

23 ICO, GDPR guidance: Contracts and liabilities between controllers and processors (Sept. 2017).

audits based on detailed specifications and required evidence. And they may utilize and assist with compliance certification efforts of the controller or processor and monitoring compliance with approved codes of conduct.

3.2.1 GDPR Compliance High-Level Checklist and Questions

Requirement	Controllers	Processors
Data processing principles (Article 5): • Lawful, fair, transparent • Purpose limitation • Data minimization • Accuracy • Storage limitation • Integrity and confidentiality • Accountability	✓	
Legal basis for processing (Articles 6–8): • Unambiguous consent • Execution of a contract • Controller's legal obligations • Vital interest of DS • Public interest • Legitimate interest	✓	
Legal basis for sensitive data (Article 9): • Explicit consent • Controller's legal obligations • Vital interest of DS • Legal claims • Public interest/health • Other	✓	
Data subject rights (Articles 12–22): • Information before collection • Access to personal data • Rectification of personal data • Erasure of personal data • Restrict processing • Portability of personal data • Object to processing • Automated processing decisions • Complain to DPA • Judicial remedies	✓	
Controller's responsibilities (Article 24)	✓	

Requirement	Controllers	Processors
Privacy by design and default (Article 25)	✔	
Processor's responsibilities (Article 28)	✔	✔
Follow controller's instructions (Article 29)		✔
Records keeping (Article 30)	✔	✔
Cooperate with DPAs (Article 31)	✔	✔
InfoSec safeguards (Article 32)	✔	✔
Data breach notification (Articles 33–34)	✔	✔
DPIA/Prior consultation (Articles 35–36)	✔	
Designate/Support DPOs (Articles 37–39)	✔	✔
Transfers outside EEA (Articles 44–49): • Adequacy • SCCs • BCRs • Privacy Shield • Explicit consent	✔	✔
Comply with other data protection laws in the EU and other jurisdictions	✔	✔
Liability for (Articles 79–84): • Administrative fines • Other penalties • Judicial damages • Criminal fines/imprisonment	✔	✔
Member state employment laws (Article 88) and GDPR-implementing laws	✔	✔

The high-level questions the DPO could ask when filling out this checklist:

- Does your organization process the personal data of EU residents?
- Which applications and systems process that personal data?
- Does each type of processing follow all the DP principles (lawful, fair, transparent; purpose limitation; data minimization; accuracy; storage limitation; integrity and confidentiality)?
- How does the controller demonstrate accountability for each of these principles?

- Does each instance of processing have a documented legal basis?
- If the basis is consent, what happens if it is withdrawn?
- Are the legal bases different for processing special categories of personal data?
- Are data subjects properly and timely informed of all relevant information concerning the legal basis?
- How does your organization respond to the exercise of each type of data subject rights?
- What measures does your (controller) organization implement to comply with its obligations under the GDPR?
- How can your organization demonstrate that compliance?
- How does your DP policy assist with compliance?
- How does your organization implement privacy by design and default (see Chapter 5)?
- Do any processors operate only under an agreement and the instructions of the controller and assist with compliance?
- What measures does your (processor) organization implement to comply with its obligations under the GDPR?
- How can your organization demonstrate that compliance?
- What records of processing are maintained?
- In what manner does your organization cooperate with all relevant DPAs?
- Are the InfoSec safeguards sufficient and effective (see Chapter 5)?
- Are the data breach response processes sufficient and effective (see Chapter 5)?
- Are the DPIA and prior consultation processes sufficient and effective (see Chapter 4)?
- Has the need for a DPO been evaluated and documented?
- Has the mandatory or voluntary DPO been appropriately designated, positioned, and tasked?

- Are all transfers of personal data outside the EEA validly done using one of the accepted safeguard mechanisms (see Chapter 6)?
- Are all EU and applicable foreign DP laws being complied with (see Chapter 6)?
- Are the specific provisions of relevant member state laws and GDPR implementing statutes understood and complied with?
- Is all staff made aware of their roles in DP compliance and trained appropriately?

3.2.2 GDPR Initial Assessment and Audits

3.2.2.1 Initial Assessments

Utilizing this first impression GDPR checklist supported by the types of documentation required to evidence each area of obligation, the DPO can gain an initial understanding of areas of GDPR noncompliance. At this point, the DPO has already interviewed senior executives and operational specialists across a wide variety of areas within the controller or processor organization, asking leading questions to identify possible areas of noncompliance. The DPO has reviewed documentation at a high level and has reviewed the existing data protection policy at a more detailed level. The DPO has either reviewed or helped to build the data and processing inventory.

With all the information available from these activities, the DPO should been able to take an initial try at filling out this GDPR-compliance checklist and questions for all major processing activities across documented areas of personal data. HR and job applicant systems, mobile apps and web applications that process and fulfill sales to individuals, digital marketing systems, email and instant messaging systems, and all IT utility software tools would be obvious candidates for systems and software that would process personal data in most organizations.

Areas of noncompliance may immediately be obvious, and where the DPO has not acquired sufficient information to determine compliance, they should seek out relevant specialists to gather that information. One trap to avoid is to assume if there is no documentation or no evidence available that the controller or processor is not compliant. Often it is the case that documentation creation and evidence building lag the implementation of new processes and businesses, so the DPO must differentiate between an area of noncompliance and an area of non-documentation. From their initial assessment, a gap analysis should detail the initial areas of noncompliance found, plus those areas that need to be documented or have evidence created. From this list, the DPO can discuss with the controller or processor what steps can be undertaken in what priority order to remediate these identified compliance gaps.

No organization can address all gaps immediately, so the focus should be on those remediation activities that do the most to reduce the risk to data subject interests, rights, and freedoms, within reasonable time and resource constraints. While the organization is working on these major risk reduction activities, the DPO should become familiar with available documentation on a more detailed level and on evidence being gathered to support compliance and the tools available to sample that evidence. At each opportunity, the DPO should be making the organization and its employees more aware of the DP responsibilities under the GDPR.

3.2.2.2 Internal Audits

After the initial compliance assessment, the DPO will be carrying out more frequent and formal internal compliance audits. The organization should be prepared for these audits based on schedules and guidance from the DPO. The DPO should specify the compliance audit objectives and processes, the types of documentation and evidence required in each area of compliance, and preliminary expectations about the findings. The operational teams and all needed specialists should be fully involved in at least the initial audits to learn how to get into and stay in compliance. Reports of the official audits should be sent to the board for review and discussion after being shared with relevant staff members to determine appropriate steps and timelines for remediation.

Under Article 39(1)(b), in monitoring and auditing the controller or processor, the DPO is looking for compliance with the GDPR, with other EU or member state data protection law (e.g., ePrivacy Directive/Regulation), and with the DP policies of the organization, specifically how DP-related responsibilities are assigned, how awareness of DP obligations and rights is raised, including use of the DP policy, and how staff is trained about these DP obligations and rights in regards to the performance of their processing of personal data.

The key differences between this initial assessment and the more formal periodic compliance audits include that the DPO will not be engaged in a fix-it-as-I-find-it mode but will be documenting compliance gaps for reporting to senior management. As such, the organization should be notified of needed remediations from the initial assessment and given time to implement those. Also, evidence must be produced instead of merely having policies and procedures, as the DPO is looking for the effectiveness of the DP risk management leading to compliance with the GDPR. Questionnaires, interviews, and verification letters may be used to ascertain whether the actual processing of personal data is different than that documented in procedures and policies.

A formalized DP audit program can be developed using procedures from the European Committee for Standardization (CEN),[24] from members organizations, such as ISACA,[25] or national auditing associations, such as the American Institute of Certified Public Accountants and Canadian Institute of Chartered Accountants.[26] Whichever method is used, the important aspects are to have specific audit objectives, to notify those who will be subject to the audit, to require evidence to back up compliance activities, to work with internal auditors who may already have techniques and knowledge that can assist the GDPR compliance audit, then to generate a formal report noting any compliance risks.

3.2.2.3 External Audits

Beyond their own audits, the DPO may be involved in an audit carried out by a DPA. The Irish Office of the DPC has published a guide to such audits with helpful appendices for self-assessment.[27] The audits carried out by the DPC focus on compliance with DP laws and its own DP policy, gaps and weaknesses, remedial actions, compliance improvements, best practice recommendations, and positive findings. Most audits are pre-arranged; use questionnaires to gather information

---

24 CEN, Personal Data Protection Audit Framework (EU Directive EC 95.46) — Part I: Baseline Framework and Part II: Checklists, questionnaires and templates for users of the framework solution.
25 ISACA, IS Audit/Assurance Program — Data Privacy.
26 AIPCA/CAC, Generally Accepted Privacy Principles.
27 DPC, Guide to Audit Process v2.0 (Aug. 2014).

around processing regarding the DP principles; and have on-site visits to view data, sensitive documents, third-party arrangements, and observations of DP practice and safeguard. A confidential audit report is produced, along with monitoring of follow-up actions.

The guide's appendices include illustrative audit questions around areas such as how data is collected from customers and employees and processed, sensitive data, service application forms, third-party requests for disclosure, staff training and awareness, marketing, contracts with data processors, access requests, computer system security, removable media, network security, biometrics, and CCTV. The self-assessment asks questions under the DP principles, records or processing, training and education, and DPOs. Common audit recommendations include establishing a compliance function, staff training and awareness, ensuring the DP principles are complied with, addressing marketing opt-ins and opt-outs, InfoSec, disclosures, retention, third-party contracts, DP policies and statements, biometrics, CCTV, and access controls. The ICO also has an audit guide[28] with appendices covering example question areas and evidence, engagement letters, and audit reports.

3.2.3 Certification under GDPR and Codes of Conduct

3.2.3.1 Certification

The compliance of a controller or processor with the GDPR may be helped by evidence of certification. Article 24(3) states a controller's adherence to a certification mechanism can be used to help demonstrate compliance with controller obligations, and Article 28(5) states a processor's adherence to a certification mechanism can be used to help demonstrate compliance with a processor's obligations. In addition, for the security requirements under Article 32 and the privacy by design requirements under Article 25, as discussed in Chapter 5, certifications may be evidence of compliance. For transfers of personal data outside the EEA under Article 47, as discussed in Chapter 6, adherence to an approved certification mechanism, along with commitments of the receiving controller or processor, can be deemed an appropriate safeguard to allow this transfer without specific DPA authorization. So, what is certification under the GDPR?

---

28 ICO, Auditing data protection — a guide to ICO data protection audits v.3.5 (June 2015).

Under Article 42, certification mechanisms and the resultant data protection marks and seals, as supporting the accountability principle, are highly encouraged to be developed by the EC, the EDPB, DPAs, and member states. These will also assist with transparency, so that data protection compliance levels of products and services can be quickly ascertained. Certification based on the developed criteria will last up to three years and be renewal but can be withdrawn if no longer meeting the criteria. Certification does not replace maintaining ongoing compliance with the GDPR. The list of certified organizations will be publicly available. Certification and renewal will happen under domain of certification bodies covered under Article 43 and criteria approved by local DPAs or national accreditation bodies for member states certifications and the EDPB if concerning EU-wide certification criteria.

ENISA has published a report[29] on the how to address certification under the GDPR and some existing certification mechanisms. It starts by identifying a startup problem, that for certification the "GDPR provisions need to be further elaborated to be fit-for-purpose for certification." It then specifies that certification in this context requires independent third-party assessment, not self-assessment (first-party) or controller assessment of a processor (second-party). It is important to note that compliance is with the compliance criteria drawn from the GDPR so there is no certification of compliance with the GDPR itself. Also, GDPR certification would only be of processing by controllers and processors, not of any products or services.

3.2.3.2 Codes of Conduct

Under Articles 40 and 41, codes of conduct drawn up by member associations of certain categories of controllers or processors serve a similar purpose to certification. Article 40 allows for the use of conducts of conduct to indicate compliance with the GDPR. These codes would be drawn up by associations that controllers or processors may belong to, for example, in a certain industry. The codes would need to address inter alia the DP principles, data subject rights, InfoSec, privacy by design, pseudonymization, the legitimate interests pursued by controllers in specific context, personal data breaches, overseas transfers, dealing with children, information provide to data subjects and the public, and dispute resolution.

---
29 ENISA, Recommendations on European Data Protection Certification (Nov. 2017).

A code must be submitted for review to the local DPA who would be the approver of a code of conduct that is applicable to a single member state. The EDPB is the approving body for a code of conduct that is applicable across several member states. The EC has the ability to be the approver of a code of conduct that would apply across the EU. Article 41 allows for a body with appropriate expertise, independence, and lack of conflicts, which has been accredited by a DPA to monitor organizations for compliance with the code of conduct and to take appropriate actions for noncompliance. The body needs to have procedures for assessing compliance and for handling complaints.

CHAPTER 4

DPO Tasks — Risk and DPIAs

The GDPR has a significant focus on understanding and addressing risk. This includes what the DPO does. Article 39(2) states "The data protection officer shall in the performance of his or her tasks have due regard to the risk associated with processing operations, taking into account the nature, scope, context and purposes of processing." So, it is critical for DPOs to have a deep understanding of what risk is, where it comes from, how it assessed in the data protection context, how risk is treated, and the concept of residual risk. Risk is an essential concept to all GDPR compliance activities, and sometimes that risk is focused on the organization and sometimes focused on the data subject.

Under Article 39(1), the DPO is required "to provide advice where requested as regards the data protection impact assessment and monitor its performance pursuant to Article 35." The WP29 has made it clear that the DPO is to be involved in DPIAs but only in the role of advising and monitoring, not actually performing the work. Unfortunately, there is no standardized format for a DPIA, so a DPO would need to understand several different methodologies, ensuring that the one used (or the combination of several) meets the requirements of Article 35 and GPDR compliance generally.

DPO Areas of Focus

- Risk management methodologies
- Risk described in the GDPR
- GDPR requirements for DPIAs
- Various DPIA methodologies

4.1 Risk[1]

Risk can be defined as the effect of uncertainty on an organization's objectives.[2] The level or magnitude of risk is the intersection of the consequences of an event affecting these objectives and the likelihood of that event occurring. Risk *identification* involves finding these events and their potential consequences. Risk *analysis* determines the level of risk based on the organization's exposure to certain events. Risk *evaluation* applies risk *criteria* to the output of the risk analysis to determine if a specific level of risk is acceptable. Risk criteria are based upon internal factors, such as the organization's objectives, policies, processes, organizational structure, decision-making processes, governance, capabilities, relationships, and information flow; and external factors, such as laws, regulations, standards, competitors, the political and financial environment, relationships, finances, and technology change. Risk *assessment* is the combination of the three steps of risk identification, risk analysis, and risk evaluation.

In the data protection law context, risk assessment is the process of identifying which external and internal *threats* and internal *vulnerabilities* combine to create *exploits* in information assets of an organization, leading to legal liabilities for the controller and damage for the data subject. External threats may originate from sources as diverse as litigation and enforcement actions to cyberattacks. Internal threats come from insiders who pursue their own agenda, such as stealing confidential information or trade secrets. Vulnerabilities may arise from a lack of employee training or awareness on data protection, from improper design of software or infrastructure, or by not fully following through on established compliance procedures. The internal and external threats can act to create an exploit that attacks an information asset through any vulnerability in the control structure of an organization. This creates a *risk* to the organization and data subject. Risks can be ordered by the potential harm caused by the risk, based upon the likelihood of its occurrence and the damage it would do to the organization and data subject. Those risks above a certain weighted level of harm are addressed by the risk treatment process to reduce identified risks.

Because the types and character of threats and vulnerabilities are

---

[1] Excerpted from Thomas J. Shaw, *Information and Internet Law — Global Practice*.
[2] ISO Guide 73, Risk management — Vocabulary (Nov. 2009).

constantly changing, it is essential that risk assessments are performed regularly. Risk assessments and treatments are often required by statutes and regulations. To understand the process of managing risk, the ISO InfoSec risk management methodology is described next. This risk methodology and others from NIST and ENISA arise primarily out of the information security and cybersecurity contexts but can be easily expanded to deal with other risks in the processing of personal data. The descriptions that follow have been supplemented to address risks beyond information security and cybersecurity risk, including more fully data protection legal risk. Risk in the data protection context extends the harm to both the controller from noncompliance and the data subject's rights, freedoms, and interests. Risk as used in the GDPR is described in the final section.

4.1.1 ISO 27005

This international standard was developed as part of the ISO 27000 series to deal with information security, first in 2008[3] and then a terminology update in 2011.[4] A risk assessment is defined as a process of risk *identification* (process of finding, recognizing, and describing risks), risk *analysis* (process to comprehend the nature of risk and to determine the level of risk, which is the magnitude of a risk, expressed in terms of the combination of consequences and their likelihood), and risk *evaluation* (process of comparing the results of risk analysis with risk criteria to determine whether the risk and/or its magnitude is acceptable or tolerable). This Risk Management Process[5] includes the phases of context establishment, risk assessment, risk treatment, and risk acceptance and ongoing interfaces with risk monitoring and review and risk communication and consultation with stakeholders.

The Context Establishment phase requires an organization to ensure that it has appropriate resources and organization structure to handle the risk management process. It defines the information assets, business processes, and business organizations that are to be within the scope of the risk management process. It requires that the organization develops

---

3 ISO/IEC 27005:2008, Information technology — Security techniques — Information security risk management (June 2008).
4 ISO/IEC 27005:2011, Information technology — Security techniques — Information security risk management (June 2011).
5 *Id.* at p. 8.

"basic" criteria, specifically those criteria that will be used to determine the criticality of information assets (risk evaluation criteria), the damage that the loss, disclosure, or impairment of these assets would entail (risk impact criteria), and risk acceptance criteria on when to accept residual risk (risk remaining after risk treatments have been applied). Risk Communication allows differing levels of risk perception among stakeholders to be exchanged and fed into and from the risk assessment phase and provides a sense of ownership of the risks identified.

Risk Assessment

The three steps of the risk assessment phase are risk identification, risk analysis, and risk evaluation. Hypothetical French undertaking Richelieu is used to briefly illustrate some of these techniques in this section from a DP perspective. Remember that this is an InfoSec methodology to which DP is being added, which means the perspective is not only risks to the organization but also the data subject.

1. Risk Identification

The identification of risk consists of identifying many different components that in total will comprise the risk inventory of an organization. These steps are the identification of assets, threats, existing controls, vulnerabilities, and consequences.

Identification of assets: This step involves inventorying assets needing protection and valuing those assets. The organization protects its assets because they have value to the organization and personal data because of its value to data subjects. This comprises information assets, business processes and practices, people, hardware/software/networks, facilities, and other business assets, such as reputation and relationships. Information assets can include items as varied as customer lists, employee data, intellectual property, and trade secrets. The customer lists and employee data would include significant amounts of personal data. Richelieu would use its data and processing inventory (see Chapter 2) to identify its personal data.

After identification of these business assets, each must be valued either quantitatively or qualitatively. Quantitative valuation can be based on traditional measures, such as original cost, depreciated cost, or cost to replace or repair. Other quantitative metrics include market value through sale, value to a competitor, legal penalties from violations of statutes or regulations, such as GDPR or contractual breaches, impacts on goodwill, competitive advantage, or customer confidence, or losses of productivity. Because monetary values are sometimes difficult to easily determine for certain business assets, like reputation, people, misuse of data, or trade secrets, qualitative scales, such as low, medium, and high, can be used. Richelieu can decide to value violations of the GDPR either in terms of administrative fines, judicial fines, or in terms on the impacts on data subjects, but it may be easiest to just use a qualitative scale of low, medium, and high.

Identification of threats: This step requires inventorying both internal and external threats, whether they are intentional, accidental, or environmental. Threats that may be unexpected, as well as those that are expected, should be included to the extent possible to foresee these. Threats lists can be derived from the organization's own experiences, from those of other organizations, from the owners of information assets, from third-party threat catalogues, internal or external legal counsel and auditors, insurance companies, the human resource or IT teams, government agencies, and current news and events.

Threats comprise a broad range from damage to facilities, cyberattacks, theft of trade secrets, natural disasters, failure of key processes, and disclosure of confidential information to litigation, regulatory violations, including lack of compliance with GDPR, loss of reputation or key employees, fraud, product or service failures, and changes to technology. DP threats to Richelieu include all InfoSec threats, employees who might steal or lose personal data, and surprisingly data subjects who may exercise their data subject rights.

Identification of existing controls: This step involves inventorying those controls that have already been implemented to deal with identified risks in previous risk assessments. Existing controls can be found by reviewing control-related documents, talking with those people responsible for operating processes implementing various controls, through performing on-site inspections and monitoring of the use of controls, and from audit reports and documentation. In addition to locating existing controls, a measure of their effectiveness must be determined. This effectiveness of a control can be determined by an evaluation of its reduction of the likeliness of a threat exploiting a control or reducing its impact. Effectiveness of controls can also be obtained from internal or external audit reports or management, legal, InfoSec, DPIAs, or DP compliance audit internal control reviews. Richelieu would likely have existing InfoSec controls, but does it have the controls in place to ensure wholesale GDPR compliance? Has its DP policy been appropriately updated for GDPR?

Identification of vulnerabilities: This step attempts to inventory those vulnerabilities in the systems and processes of an organization that could allow a threat to exploit it and cause harm to the organization. Vulnerabilities that do not have threats to exploit them may not require controls, as improperly designed or implemented controls may lead to new vulnerabilities. Areas where vulnerabilities may exist include organization, processes and procedures, management routines, personnel, physical environment, information system configuration, hardware, software or communications equipment, dependence on external parties, contracts, intellectual property protections, training, or insurance.

Methods of identifying vulnerabilities include DP compliance audits as in Chapter 3, DPIAs in Chapter 4, code reviews for developed software, automated scanning tools for purchased software, network penetration tests for cyberattacks, security test scripts for infrastructure, walk-throughs for business continuity and disaster recovery plans, and legal reviews of contractual provisions, insurance, and intellectual property, plus using interviews and questionnaires to stakeholders, physical inspection, and document analysis. Richelieu may be missing or have outdated InfoSec controls, it may not have implemented sufficient GDPR awareness raising and training, or it may have not implemented processes to deal with the exercise of data subject rights or keeping accurate records of processing of personal data.

Identification of consequences: This step determines the consequences that arise when threats do exploit vulnerabilities resulting in an incident that impacts an information asset. The consequences can involve the time and expense to investigate and resolve an incident, the impact of the incident on work productivity, DPA administrative fines or data subject judicial awards, business opportunities lost because of the incident, any health and safety impacts, the financials costs, any new legal liabilities or exposures, emotional or psychological costs, discrimination, loss of an individual's privacy, self-determination, freedom of expression, or movement, loss of trust, and the impacts on an organization's reputation, goodwill, and its future plans.

Consequences may be temporary or permanent in nature. The various scenarios where incidents arise and their impact costs on business processes and assets, determined in the context establishment step, should be documented for use in succeeding steps. When InfoSec threats take advantage of vulnerabilities in Richelieu's software patching, this can lead to unauthorized disclosure of personal data. When data subjects exercise their rights, the lack of training of employees or access rights response processes could lead to delay and possibly the wrong or insufficient personal data being returned to data subject. Lack of records of processing could bring compliance fines.

2. Risk Analysis

There are several steps in risk analysis, starting with determining the type of risk analysis methodology to use. This is a choice between looking at risk in either qualitative or quantitative ways or both. In qualitative analysis, a scale, such as high, medium, or low, is applied to the magnitude of potential consequences and the likelihood that they will occur. This type of analysis is appropriate for an initial screening of risks or when there is not sufficient quantitative data available. Quantitative analysis uses data, most likely historical data of incidents, to estimate the magnitude of potential consequences and the likelihood that they will occur. The validity of this analysis technique depends upon the accuracy of the data. The use of historical data implies that new types of threats may not be incorporated. The uncertainty and variability of the potential consequences and the likelihood of their occurrence should be considered when performing the risk analysis.

The three steps in risk analysis are assessment of the consequences, assessment of incident likelihood, and determination of the level of risk. When performing the first step of assessing the consequences of an incident, the replacement cost and the business or legal impact of the loss, disclosure, unavailability, or infringement of an information asset are used. The consequences can use either based on extrapolation from past data or studies or from models of outcomes of events and can be expressed in terms of monetary, technical, legal, or human impact criteria. At a minimum, there will be financial, technical, and legal costs to respond to each incident scenario, even if the longer-term business consequences are not significant. Again, depending on the type of violation of the GDPR, Richelieu would have to consider and apply some measure of the financial and legal consequences to the organization and the financial and emotional consequences to data subjects.

The second step of incident likelihood considers how often threats occur and how easily vulnerabilities are exploited. This consideration will take into account the organization's experience with the likelihood of threats and any available statistics; the motivation, capabilities, and resources available to possible attackers; the perceived attractiveness and vulnerability of information assets; newness of regulations, such as the GDPR, and related training and awareness programs; proximity to and possibility of unstable situations and other factors influencing accidents, such as human error and malfunction of equipment, individual and collective vulnerabilities of the organization's processes and people, and effectiveness of existing controls. Richelieu could look to its own compliance history and all the steps it has taken to become compliant with the GDPR and any gaps raised in the initial assessment or compliance audits by the DPO.

The third step of determining the level of risk is made by combining the outputs of the prior two steps, the consequences of incidents and their likelihood. So, the consequences of each type of incident can be charted against the combined likelihood of the occurrence of a threat and the ease of exploitation of a vulnerability. If the qualitative measures of high, medium, and low are applied to threats and vulnerabilities, then there are nine possible combinations (from low- threat occurrence-low ease of vulnerability exploitation to high-threat occurrence-high ease of vulnerability exploitation) that can be charted against the various levels of financial and legal consequences.

Richelieu's consequence of noncompliance with the GDPR may be administrative fines but the likelihood is low considering the steps taken and the regulatory posture of the local DPA. The risk to a data subject may be more or less significant. A delay in receiving a subject access request may have little risk to a data subject, while the unauthorized disclosure of a biometric data from a vulnerability caused by unpatched software could have be considered high risk. The level of risk from not keeping accurate records of processing could be high, combining high likelihood of a finding of noncompliance with the high consequence of an administrative fine.

Those incident scenarios intersecting the lowest financial and legal consequences with the low-threat occurrence-low ease of vulnerability exploitation would have the lowest risk ratings, while the incident scenarios intersecting the highest financial and legal consequences with the high-threat occurrence-high ease of vulnerability exploitation would have the highest risk ratings. In other words, the less likely incident scenarios that have the least business impact would be assigned the lowest risk ratings and the most likely incident scenarios that have the largest business, and data subject impact would be assigned the highest risk ratings.

3. Risk Evaluation

The levels of risk for each incident scenario determined in the final step of risk assessment will feed into the risk evaluation step. The levels of risk are then assessed by the risk evaluation criteria originally developed during context establishment. The risk evaluation criteria are based on considerations, such as:

- Data subject perceptions and reactions.
- The strategic value of the business information process.
- The criticality of the information assets involved.
- Legal and regulatory requirements, and contractual obligations.
- Operational and business importance of availability, confidentiality, and integrity.
- Stakeholders expectations and perceptions, and negative consequences for goodwill and reputation.

When evaluating the incident scenarios against the risk evaluation criteria, factors, such as the confidence in the risk identification and analysis steps, applicability of certain risks to the current business activities of the organization, and the consolidation of smaller risks into larger ones, are considered. The legal, regulatory, and contractual requirements also should be factored in to the estimated risks. The output of this process will be a list of risk-prioritized incident scenarios to which risk treatments can be considered, for those activities deemed appropriate to undertake (risk evaluation may indicate that the risk of certain activities is so high that the activity itself should not be undertaken). The current circumstances and future expectations and business plans of the organization and legal exposures will always be of paramount importance in performing a risk evaluation. For Richelieu, the disclosure of biometric data would prioritize highest, administrative fines for not keeping records of processing would be in the middle, and a slight delay in responding to a SAR would be lowest.

Risk Treatment

The prioritized list of risks that is the result of the risk assessment phase then leads into the risk treatment phase. Risk treatment is the process of examining each of the incident scenarios previously identified and choosing one of four appropriate actions to address the risks. These options are to reduce the risk by applying a control to the risk, to retain the individual risks, to avoid these risks by modifying behavior or processes, or to transfer the risk to an outside party. These various actions will be undertaken based on their respective costs and benefits to as low a level of risk as reasonable. High impact risks that are infrequent or unlikely may necessitate controls due to the significant consequences. When the risk treatment plan has been developed for all incident scenarios within scope, the residual risk for the organization after applying risk treatments must be analyzed to determine if it is within an acceptance range for the organization's risk acceptance criteria.

1. Risk Reduction

Risk is reduced through the application of controls into the incident scenarios to minimize the threats or vulnerabilities. Controls are combinations of automated and manual procedures that deal with threats before or after they exploit vulnerabilities. Controls can perform the following functions: correction, elimination, prevention, impact minimization, deterrence, detection, recovery, monitoring, and awareness. Noncompliance with statutory, regulatory, and contractual obligations is one significant risk area where controls would be applied. While it would seem ideal to eliminate all risk through controls, this approach is constrained by limits, such as time, finances, technology, operations, legality, and complexity. In ISO information security risk management, ISO 27002 contains a list of controls that can be applied to treat identified risks.[6] Richelieu could determine that it needs to review its software patch procedures, implement more GDPR training, accurately record processing, and designate a full-time DPO to monitor for compliance.

2. Risk Retention

Incident scenario risk that does not exceed the organization's risk criteria may not need any or additional controls and can be retained (not treated). If the response to subject access requests takes 20 days instead of the expected 10 days, this is still compliant with the GDPR and so the risk of this delay could be retained by Richelieu.

3. Risk Avoidance

Certain activities that lead to the incident scenarios could be curtailed or eliminated. Not all activities are essential to perform by doing certain processing activities in a different way, or not at all risk can be reduced. Richelieu could reexamine why it is collecting biometric data in the first place and find a different way to accomplish the same business objective, avoiding this DP risk.

4. Risk Transfer

Risk can be transferred when the risks are insured through various types of insurance coverage or when the activity itself is outsourced to a service provider. The transferring of risk to external parties may create new risks, such as the loss of certain internal expertise or the ability of the outsourcing provider as a going-concern in the location of the outsourced service. The transfer of outsourced duties outside the organization will still mean that the ultimate legal responsibility for those risks remains with the organization, subject to certain contractual liability and indemnification provisions. Although a controller cannot transfer their obligations under the GDPR, Richelieu may, for example, engage a processor with a best practices data center to store the personal data they collect from customers and avoid another DP risk by requiring that it stores data only within the EEA.

When these four methods have been applied to the risks of the incident scenarios, the residual risk must be determined and either

---

6 ISO/IEC 27002:2013, Information Technology — Security Techniques — Code of Practice for Information Security Controls (Oct. 2013).

accepted or additional risk treatments must be implemented to get the residual risk to an acceptable level. Richelieu would have to reassess its processes if there is a residual risk of noncompliance not allowed for under the GDPR and national law derogations.

To avoid this level of residual risk, the organization could break the incident response scenario into those actions they will do in any situation and those that are specific to the circumstances of each incident. To address the former, processes can be designed and implemented to recognize and categorize an incident, deploy resources, and contain and respond to any type of incident. Employees can be trained on those processes, and others can be given awareness training. The benefit of lower residual risk by avoiding bad outcomes associated with a delayed incident response may outweigh the costs involved in implementing and training on the new processes. The residual risk would then compromise just the fact-specific responses for each incident, which may now be acceptable to the organization.

Risk Monitoring and Review requires ongoing analysis of the results of the risk treatments implemented and changes proposed for those that are not performing as expected. The business environment must also be continually assessed, addressing the legal and environmental context, competition context, risk assessment approach, asset value and categories, impact criteria, risk evaluation criteria, risk acceptance criteria, total cost of ownership, and necessary resources. Legal and business threats may arise, or vulnerabilities may be introduced at any time from any direction, so constant vigilance is required. The organization's business strategy, objectives, and structure are subject to change over time, and, to stay relevant, the risk management structure must adapt accordingly.

4.1.2 Risk in the GDPR

Risk awareness in general and risk management processes specifically have taken an increasingly larger role in legislation, especially as it concerns the rights of individuals or consumers. As privacy and consumer laws are being revised globally, risk-based analysis and protections based upon risk are becoming more widespread. Enforcement of the requirements to address potential harm using risk-aware processes is part of enforcement actions and litigation.

Risk awareness and assessment is required by statute in an increasing number of jurisdictions or when revising existing laws. Under the GDPR,[7] risk is mentioned 75 times in the text of the document, a significant increase over the law it replaced, the Data Protection Directive. Importantly, addressing risk is required in the following provisions (emphasis added):

- *Role of controller*: "Taking into account the nature, scope, context and purposes of processing as well as the *risks* of varying likelihood and severity for the rights and freedoms of natural persons, the controller shall implement appropriate technical and organisational measures."[8]

- *Privacy by design*: "Taking into account… the *risks* of varying likelihood and severity for rights and freedoms of natural persons posed by the processing, the controller shall… implement appropriate technical and organisational measures… which are designed to implement data-protection principles."

- *Security of processing*: "the controller and the processor shall implement appropriate technical and organisational measures to ensure a level of security appropriate to the *risk*... In assessing the appropriate level of security account shall be taken in particular of the *risks* that are presented by processing."[9]

- *Personal data breach*: "In the case of a personal data breach, the controller shall without undue delay… notify… unless the personal data breach is unlikely to result in a *risk* to the rights and freedoms of natural persons."[10]

- *Personal data breach*: "When the personal data breach is likely to result in a high *risk* to the rights and freedoms of natural persons, the controller shall communicate the personal data breach to the data subject without undue delay."[11]

---

7 Regulation (EU) 2016/679 of the European Parliament and of the Council of 27 April 2016 on the protection of natural persons with regard to the processing of personal data and on the free movement of such data, and repealing Directive 95/46/EC (General Data Protection Regulation).
8 *Id.* Art. 24.
9 *Id.* Art. 32.
10 *Id.* Art. 33.
11 *Id.* Art. 34.

- *Data protection impact statement*: "Where necessary, the controller shall carry out a review to assess if processing is performed in accordance with the data protection impact assessment at least when there is a change of the *risk* represented by processing operations."[12]

- *Prior consultation*: "The controller shall consult the supervisory authority prior to processing where a data protection impact assessment under Article 35 indicates that the processing would result in a high *risk* in the absence of measures taken by the controller to mitigate the *risk*."[13]

- *Data protection officer*: "The data protection officer shall in the performance of his or her tasks have due regard to the *risk* associated with processing operations."[14]

- *Derogations for transfers outside the EEA*: "the data subject has explicitly consented to the proposed transfer, after having been informed of the possible *risks* of such transfers for the data subject due to the absence of an adequacy decision and appropriate safeguards."[15]

- *Supervisory authority*: "each supervisory authority shall on its territory… promote public awareness and understanding of the *risks*, rules, safeguards and rights in relation to processing."[16]

- *European Data Protection Board*: "as to the circumstances in which a personal data breach is likely to result in a high *risk* to the rights and freedoms of the natural persons."[17]

4.2 Data Protection Impact Assessments

Data protection impact assessments (DPIAs), also referred to as privacy impact assessments (PIAs), look at the processing of controllers and processors. Unlike an InfoSec assessment that would be focusing on the

---

12 *Id.* Art. 35.
13 *Id.* Art. 36.
14 *Id.* Art. 39.
15 *Id.* Art. 49.
16 *Id.* Art. 57.
17 *Id.* Art. 70.

risk to the organization from a breach of confidentiality, integrity, and accessibility of data, DPIAs take the view of the data subject and the risk to the data subject from a failure by the controller or processor to be stay in compliance with all its GDPR obligations. Because there is no universal standard for DPIAs, after looking at the statutory requirements, this section will discuss recommended methodologies from several sources: the ICO in the U.K., CNIL in France, the U.S. government, and the ISO.

4.2.1 GDPR

4.2.1.1 Requirements

Under Article 35, controllers are required to perform a DPIA in certain situations. This occurs when processing, especially that dealing with new technologies, "is likely to result in a high risk to the rights and freedoms of natural persons." The DPIA is to be carried out before processing starts and be done in consultation with the DPO. DPIAs for processing existing when the GDPR comes into effect are optional unless new risks arise. DPIAs are required in three situations:

- "a systematic and extensive evaluation of personal aspects relating to natural persons which is based on automated processing, including profiling, and on which decisions are based that produce legal effects concerning the natural person or similarly significantly affect the natural person;

- processing on a large scale of special categories of data referred to in Article 9(1), or of personal data relating to criminal convictions and offences referred to in Article 10; or

- a systematic monitoring of a publicly accessible area on a large scale."

DPAs in each member state are to derive lists of those processing operations that require a DPIA and those that do not and everything not on those lists will have to be evaluated by each controller. If there is a change in risk, the controller must review whether the actual processing is being done in accordance with the DPIA. Controllers should also seek the views of data subjects as part of the DPIA if appropriate and document why such views were not sought.

At a minimum, the DPIA is to contain:

- Description of the processing and the purposes thereof.
- Assessment of the necessity and proportionality of the processing for these purposes.
- Assessment of the risks to the rights and freedoms of data subjects.
- Description of the safeguards that protect the personal data and ensure GDPR compliance.

If a DPIA shows that there may be a high risk of to the rights and freedoms of data subjects after applying the safeguards (residual risk), the controller is required under Article 36 to consult with the DPA by providing the DPIA along with other information and then possibly take advice from the DPA on how to address the risk in this processing.

4.2.1.2 Guidelines

The WP29 has published guidelines for DPIAs under the GDPR.[18] This starts off by emphasizing that controllers who do not perform a DPIA, who do so incorrectly (including not consulting with the DPO), or who do not consult with the DPA when required are subject to administrative fines up to two percent of global revenue. Also, DPIAs done by the makers of hardware and software can inform but not replace a DPIA done by the purchasing controller.

The WP29 listed nine criteria that should inform the decision to carry out a DPIA. As a rule of thumb (but not definitive), if two or more criteria are met, then a DPIA is likely required. As mentioned above, member state DPAs are required to further develop these lists and send them to the EDPB, so in the future, there may be a more comprehensive list. The WP29 suggested that other criteria could be the processing of any biometric data or the personal data of children:

- Evaluation or scoring, including profiling and predicting.
    - Automated decision making with legal or similar significant effect.

---

18 Art. 29 DP WP, Guidelines on Data Protection Impact Assessment (DPIA) and determining whether processing is "likely to result in a high risk" for the purposes of Regulation 2016/679, r1 (Oct. 2017).

- Systematic monitoring.
- Sensitive data or data of a highly personal nature.
- Data processed on a large scale.
- Matching or combining datasets.
- Data concerning vulnerable data subjects.
- Innovative use or applying technological or organizational solutions.
- When the processing prevents data subjects from exercising a right or using a service or a contract.

The DPIA, done with the assistance of the processor if there is one, should be seen as a "continual process, not a one-time exercise" that starts as early in the design stage as possible and is revised even after processing has begun as the risks may change. Risk changes from processing operations include in the "data collected, purposes, functionalities, personal data processed, recipients, data combinations, risks (supporting assets, risk sources, potential impacts, threats, etc.), security measures and international transfers."

The WP29 views DPIAs as being a seven-stage iterative process:

- Description of the envisaged processing.
- Assessment of the necessity and proportionality.
- Measures already envisaged (to demonstrate compliance).
- Assessment of the risks to the rights and freedoms.
- Measures envisaged to address the risks.
- Documentation.
- Monitoring and review.

The risk assessment stage should follow standard international risk management steps by establishing the context, assessing the likelihood and severity of the consequence of an event causing a high risk to the rights and freedoms of individuals, and treating the risk. These rights and freedom can extend beyond privacy to the rights of expression, thought, movement, liberty, conscience, and religion, and prohibition of discrimination.

While the DPO should provide advice before the start of the DPIA, they should also monitor the progress of the DPIA. Additionally, the DPO "could suggest that the controller carries out a DPIA on a specific processing operation, and should help the stakeholders on the methodology, help to evaluate the quality of the risk assessment and whether the residual risk is acceptable, and to develop knowledge specific to the data controller context."

4.2.2 Methodologies

4.2.2.1 WP29

A set of common criteria was developed for any DPIA methodology that would successfully evaluate compliance with the GDPR. In Annex 2,[19] the criteria for an acceptable DPIA methodology would require all the following:

- Systematic description of the processing:
    - Nature, scope, context, and purposes of processing.
    - Personal data, recipients, and retention periods.
    - Functional processing description.
    - IT and people assets supporting personal data.
- Necessity and proportionality assessment:
    - Measures contributing to proportionality and necessity.
    - Measures contributing to DS rights.
- Risk management for DS rights and freedoms:
    - Impacts from risk sources of illegitimate access, undesired modification, and disappearance of data.
    - Severity and likelihood of impacts from identified threats.
    - Risk treatment measures.
- Involvement of DPO and DSes.

---
19 Id.

4.2.2.2 ICO

This guidance[20] for PIAs focuses on the local implementation of the DPD, under which DPIAs were not a requirement. The ICO recommended PIAs for new projects and systems and existing systems that were undergoing change but unchanged existing systems only when the finds of the PIA could be implemented. The purpose of the PIA is to reduce the privacy risks of unconsented disclosure, inaccuracies, excessive collection or retention, or misuse of personal data. These risks are manifested in damages or distress to individuals or reputational and financial risks to any organization from a data breach.

The PIA should include the following steps, including consulting with appropriate specialists and owners:

- Identifying the need for the PIA: Documenting the benefits and determining the need through screening questions:
  - Will the project involve the collection of new information about individuals?
  - Will the project compel individuals to provide information about themselves?
  - Will information about individuals be disclosed to organizations or people who have not previously had routine access to the information?
  - Are you using information about individuals for a purpose it is not currently used for or in a way it is not currently used?
  - Does the project involve you using new technology that might be perceived as being privacy intrusive (e.g., biometrics or facial recognition)?
  - Will the project result in you making decisions or taking action against individuals in ways which can have a significant impact on them?
  - Is the information about individuals of a kind particularly likely to raise privacy concerns or expectations (e.g., health or criminal records or particularly private data)?

---

20 ICO, Conducting privacy impact assessments code of practice (Feb. 2014).

- Will the project require you to contact individuals in ways which they may find intrusive?

- *Describing information flows*: How is personal data collected, stored, used, and deleted, who is it disclosed to, and what is the purpose of the processing?

- *Identifying privacy and related risk*: Privacy issues raise risks to individuals and organizations (compliance and other risks). Risk registers can record the risk, likelihood, and impact.

- *Identifying and evaluating privacy solutions*: Treat the identified risks to reduce, eliminate, or retain them. Risk treatments should be added to the risk register. Residual risk should be evaluated to determine if they are acceptable.

- *Signing off and recording the PIA outcomes*: Documenting the acceptance of the treatments and residual risk and the necessary solutions.

- *Integrating the PIA outcomes back into the project plan*: So that the risk treatment solutions are implemented.

4.2.2.3 CNIL

The CNIL in France has produced a three-volume series of PIAs. The first volume covers the PIA methodology,[21] the second PIA tools with which to carry out the methodology,[22] and good practice risk treatments measures.[23] The methodology uses four stages: context of the processing, controls to comply with legal requirements and address privacy risks, assessing privacy risks, and decision. It rests upon the two pillars of fundamental principles and rights and management of data subjects' privacy risks.

1. Context
   1.1 General description of processing and its purposes and the controller and any processors
   1.2 Detailed description of the personal data, its recipients, and its retention periods

---

21 CNIL, Methodology (how to carry out a PIA) (June 2015).
22 CNIL, Tools (templates and knowledge bases) (June 2015).
23 CNIL, Measures for the Privacy Risk Treatment (June 2012).

2. Controls
    2.1 Legal controls for compliance, such as purpose, minimization, quality, information, consent, etc.
    2.2 Organizational (e.g., policies), logical security (e.g., anonymization), and physical security (e.g., access) controls
3. Risk
    3.1 Sources of risk
    3.2 Feared events impact and severity
    3.3 Threats to personal data supporting assets leading to feared events
    3.4 Risk level based on severity and likelihood of threats
4. Decision
    4.1 Evaluate the PIA
    4.2 If not acceptable, repeat prior steps
    4.3 If acceptable, create action plan for planned controls
    4.4 Validate the PIA

The catalog of good practices has five sections. The first section, Protecting Primary Assets, includes: minimizing personal data; managing retention periods; obtaining consent; exercising data subject rights; and partitioning, anonymizing, and encrypting personal data. Addressing the Impacts includes backing up and protecting personal data and tracking IT system activity. Addressing Sources of Risk includes avoiding sources of risk, managing logical access controls, and third parties. Protecting Support Assets includes hardware, software, network, and individuals' vulnerabilities. Cross-Organizational Actions includes managing privacy protection policy and privacy risks.

The CNIL methodology also had the format a PIA report that had an introduction; a body made up of the list of legal and risk controls and a risk map; conclusion for validation; and appendices that detailed the scope, controls, risks, and action plan. Most recently, CNIL has also released an open-source software tool to be used to perform a DPIA,[24] facilitating accountability for controllers.

---

24 CNIL, analys d'impact sur la protection de donnees (Dec. 2017).

4.2.2.4 U.S.

The U.S. government, under the E-Government Act of 2002,[25] required PIAs from government agencies when developing or procuring IT systems containing PII of the public or initiating an electronic collection of PII. This is preceded by a Privacy Threshold Analysis (PTA) to determine if a PIA is required. The PTA would ask such questions as from whom data is collected, what types of personal data is collected, how such data is shared, if the data is merged, and if any determinations that have been made as to the InfoSec aspects of the system.[26]

The Privacy Act requirements include the rights to receive timely notice of location, routine use, storage, retrievability, access controls, retention, and disposal; rights of access and change to personal information; consent to disclosure; and maintenance of accurate, relevant, timely, and complete records.27 As such, the PIA will describe in the detail the information collected or maintained, the sources of that information, the uses and possible disclosures, and potential threats to the information. The uses that the information is put to by the system are described next, including the legal authority for collecting the data, the retention periods and eventual destruction, and any potential threats based on its use. Also included are any information dissemination and the controls used, the rights listed above, the information security program used, and compliance with the Privacy Act.[28]

Under implementation guidance, the following were reasons were for initiating a PIA:[29]

- Collection of new information about individuals whether compelled or voluntary.

- Conversion of records from paper-based to electronic format.

- Conversion of information from anonymous to identifiable format.

---

25 Pub. L. 107-347 (Dec. 2002).
26 *See e.g.*, U.S. Department of Homeland Security, Privacy Threshold Analysis (Sept. 2015).
27 5 U.S.C. § 552a(d)–(e).
28 *See e.g.*, U.S. Department of Homeland Security, Privacy Impact Assessment for ECS (Jan. 2013).
29 OMB Mem. M-03-22, Guidance for Implementing the Privacy Provisions of the E-Government Act (Sept. 2003).

- System management changes involving significant new uses and/or application of new technologies.

- Significant merging, matching, or other manipulation of multiple databases containing PII.

- Application of user-authentication technology to a publicly accessible system.

- Incorporation into existing databases of PII obtained from commercial or public sources.

- Significant new inter-agency exchanges or uses of PII.

- Alteration of a business process resulting in significant new collection, use, and/or disclosure of PII.

- Alteration of the character of PII due to the addition of qualitatively new types of PII.

- Implementation of projects using third-party service providers.

4.2.2.5 ISO

ISO 29134[30] is a set of guidelines for the process of running a PIA and the structure of the resulting report. It is not a standard for PIAs, unlike, say, a standard for information security. These guidelines define a PIA as a process for identifying and treating, in consultation with stakeholders, risks to personally identifiable information (PII) in a process, system, application, or device. It reiterated that PIAs are important not only for controllers and their processors but also the suppliers of digitally connected devices and that the PIA starts at the earliest design phase and continues until after implementation.

The process first involves a threshold analysis to determine if a PIA is needed, then preparing for a PIA, performing a PIA, and following up on the PIA. The Performing phase consists of the five steps:

- Identifying information flows of PII.

- Analyzing the implications of the use case.

- Determining the relevant privacy safeguarding requirements.

---

30 ISO/IEC 29134:2017, Information technology — Security techniques — Guidelines for privacy impact assessment (June 2017).

- Assessing privacy risk (using steps of risk identification, risk analysis, and risk evaluation).
- Preparing to treat privacy risk (by choosing the privacy risk treatment option; determine the controls using control sets, such as available in ISO/IEC 27002 and ISO/IEC 29151; and creating privacy risk treatment plans).

The Following Up phase consists of:

- Preparing and publishing the PIA report.
- Implementing the privacy risk treatment plan.
- Reviewing the PIA and reflecting changes to the process.

The structure of the PIA report should include sections on scope of the assessment, privacy requirements, risk assessment, risk treatment plan, and conclusions and decisions. The risk assessment includes discussion of the risk sources, threats and their likelihood, consequences and their level of impact, risk evaluation, and compliance analysis. There should also be a summary that can be made public.

CHAPTER 5

DPO Tasks — Technical Assessments

As part of evaluating compliance with the GDPR, there are certain areas that require a level of technical competence for the DPO to be able to assess. These areas requiring technical assessments are requirements in Article 32 for security of personal data, Article 25 for privacy by design and default, and Articles 33–34 for data breach response. For a DPO to assess the compliance in these areas requires certain IT knowledge and experience, which was why the DPO skills discussed in Chapter 1, including programming and IT experience. This chapter describes these technical assessments in a manner so any DPO can be involved. Anonymization of personal data is also covered.

Beyond the GDPR compliance, risk, DPIAs, and technical assessments covered in Chapters 3–5, there are other tasks DPOs must undertake. Some of these are spelled out under the GDPR, while others are implicit in the wording, and still others are best practices that benefit all her/his stakeholders. These range across a wide spectrum, from training and raising awareness on data protection with the employees of the controllers and processors and working with data subjects and DPAs to helping controllers and processors to set up processes to deal with data subjects' rights. To assist and advise on these areas does not require knowledge beyond the GDPR and general business and interpersonal skills, so will not be discussed further.

DPO Areas of Focus

- Assess InfoSec programs
- Advise on anonymization procedures
- Assess data breach response processes
- Advise on privacy by default and design

5.1 Information Security and Anonymization

Article 32 requires the controller and processor to implement, test, assess, and evaluate the effectiveness of "appropriate technical and organizational measures" considering the risks to the rights and freedoms of data subjects and the risks of processing from the "destruction, loss, alteration, unauthorized disclosure of or access to personal data." The measures, including encryption, should ensure confidentiality, integrity, availability, and resilience of processing systems and services and the rapid restoration of availability and access to personal data.

To understand InfoSec at a level sufficient to assess it independently and determine whether it complies, as a DPO must be able to do, it is best to study InfoSec certification processes and control catalogs. By seeing how an InfoSec program is certified to standard and what types of controls can be implemented to treat various risks, the InfoSec risks themselves become more clearly articulated. DPOs should look for the establishment of a rigorous InfoSec program by evaluating it using the process below, which, in turn, is based on the controls implemented from the control catalogs. The absence of or lack of documentation on every control listed in these catalogs or any variation should be explained by the controller or processor organization.

5.1.1 ISO

5.1.1.1 Process

The ISO 27001 standard[1] provides a process for the certification of an information security management system (ISMS). It does so by establishing, implementing, maintaining, and continually improving an ISMS. The ISMS was established by an organization as a means to preserve the confidentiality, integrity, and availability of information by applying a risk management process. It does this in several categories in each documented evidence must be produced that the organization is complying with the specified requirement.

The first category describes the internal and external issues of the organization and legal, regulatory and contractual requirements of interested parties, which, together with any dependencies on activities performed by other organizations, help to provide the scope of the ISMS for it to be established, implemented, maintained, and continually improved.

The second category concerns the organization's management and their demonstration of leadership and commitment, the organization's InfoSec policy, and InfoSec roles. The leadership and commitment are demonstrated by:

- Ensuring the InfoSec policy and objectives are established and compatible with the organization's strategic direction.
- Ensuring the integration of the ISMS' requirements into the organization's processes.
- Ensuring the resources needed for the ISMS are available.
- Communicating the importance of effective ISM and of conforming to the ISMS requirements.
- Ensuring that the ISMS achieves its intended outcome(s).
- Directing and supporting persons to contribute to the effectiveness of the ISMS.
- Promoting continual improvement.

---

[1] ISO/IEC 27001:2013, Information technology — Security techniques — Information security management systems — Requirements (Oct. 2013).

- Supporting other relevant management roles to demonstrate their leadership as it applies to their areas of responsibilityTop management must establish an appropriate IS policy with InfoSec objectives and commitments to any InfoSec requirements and continual improvement of the ISMS that is communicated internally and externally as appropriate. Top management also must establish the responsibilities and authorities for InfoSec roles, including adherence to this ISO standard and reporting on ISMS performance top management.

The third category involves the planning for risk assessment and risk treatment processes and IS objectives. The organization must define an IS risk assessment process that establishes risk assessment and acceptance criteria, identifies IS risks (loss of CIA) and risk owners, analyzes the consequences and likelihood of materialized risks, and evaluates the risks by comparing the level of risk from the analysis with the previously defined risk criteria and prioritizes the risks for risk treatment.

The organization then must define an InfoSec risk treatment process that determines appropriate risk treatment options based on the assessment and determines the necessary controls, documenting why controls were included or excluded from the ISO 27002 catalog. A risk treatment plan must be formulated that the risk owners agree to, including the acceptance of residual InfoSec risks. The organization then must establish measurable InfoSec objectives based on the InfoSec policy, InfoSec requirements, and results of the risk assessments and treatments. The plan to achieve the InfoSec objectives should include what will be done, with what resources, by whom, by when, and how the results will be evaluated.

The fourth category involves support, including the necessary resources to maintain the ISMS and the competence of the InfoSec-related personnel, awareness of the InfoSec policy among employees and contractors and how they contribute to ISMS effectiveness or non-conformance, need for ISMS communications, and documented information for compliance with this standard.

The fifth category covers operations, such as performing risk assessments periodically and, when there are significant changes, implementing risk treatment plans and plans for InfoSec objectives and requirements, and, in every case, documenting the results. The organization should control changes and any outsourcing.

The sixth category concerns performance evaluation of the effectiveness of the ISMS and IS performance. The organization must determine what InfoSec processes and controls to monitor and measure, how, when, and who will monitor and measure and by whom and when will the evaluation be done. Regular internal audits are required to determine conformance of the ISMS to this standard and whether it is being effectively implemented and maintained. Periodic management reviews should review all this information, plus any changes in internal or external issues and continual improvement opportunities.

The seventh and final category deals with improvements, such as addressing nonconformities, including controlling and correcting it and dealing with the consequences and then eliminating the causes of the nonconformity. The organization should continually improve the suitability, adequacy, and effectiveness of the ISMS.

5.1.1.2 Controls

The ISO 27002 standard[2] provides a catalog of controls used in the certification of an ISMS under the ISO 27001 standard. The controls are used as part of the risk treatment plan described above. They are grouped into the following 14 categories, with the applicable control objectives and individual controls:

Information security policies: The policy provides documentation and communication of management's direction and support for InfoSec in response to both business and legal requirements.

Organization of information security: The internal organization is to have roles defined and duties segregated, to avoid the possibility of unauthorized modification or misuse of information. Policies and controls are to be implemented to control both those remotely accessing information and for information on mobile devices.

Human resource security: Employees and contractors are screened and made aware of the InfoSec responsibilities and disciplined for breaching InfoSec procedures. Rules are defined for departing or role-changing employees and contractors.

---

2 ISO/IEC 27002:2013, Information technology — Security Techniques — Code of practice for information security controls (Oct. 2013).

Asset management: Information assets need to be identified, inventoried, and owned, used under an acceptable use policy, and returned when upon termination of service. To protect information, it needs to be classified, then labeled and handled in accordance with the classification. Media that contains information needs to be protected against unauthorized access when moved, removable media need to be protected based on the classification of the information, and all media need to be disposed securely.

Access control: An access control policy needs to be established, access to information and application restricted in accordance with it, and access to the organization's network and networked services only for authorized users. There should be formal processes for user registration, access rights, and secret authentication information, which should be removed upon termination of services. Privileged access rights and utility programs should be restricted and controlled. Asset owners should review user access rights periodically. Users should be accountable for their secret authentication information. There should be a secure log-on process, password management system, and restricted access to application source code.

Cryptography: So that there is effective use of encryption, there need to be policies on encryption controls and the use and protection of encryption keys and how long they will be used.

Physical and environmental security: To prevent access to physical facilities, there needs to be perimeter, office/facility, delivery areas, and physical entry controls established. Environmental and external threats, like natural disasters, attacks, or accidents, need to have physical protections designed for. To protect against loss or damage, equipment needs to be appropriately sited, maintained, not left unattended and secure disposed, protected from power failures and interception over cables, and off-site equipment needs appropriate security. Clear desk and screen policies should be adopted.

Operations security: There should be documented operating procedures, including for change and capacity management and separate development, test, and production environments. There needs to be regular backups, malware protection, regular logging of events, and software distribution processes, including user restrictions. Technical vulnerability information should be obtained and timely remediations applied and audits planned to avoid disruptions.

Communications security: To protect information and applications accessible by networks, controls should be implemented, including in network service agreements, and groups of users, information, and services appropriately segregated. Information transferred by network internally or externally should be done according to a formal policy or agreement, confidentiality or nondisclosure agreements identified, and messaging systems protected.

System acquisition, development, and maintenance: InfoSec requirements are to be included in new or enhanced system projects. Information in application services sent over public networks or involving application services transactions is to be protected. Rules for secure development of software and systems should be established, along with formal change control procedures. The development environment should be secured, outsourced development supervised, test data controlled, and system acceptance testing performed.

Supplier relationships: Security requirements must be established with suppliers through policies and agreements, services monitored, and changes managed.

InfoSec incident management: Procedures and responsibilities for incident response must be established, InfoSec weaknesses reported, incidents responded to, evidence collected, and lessons learned to avoid similar future incidents.

InfoSec aspects of business continuity management: InfoSec needs during business interruptions should be planned for, implemented, and reviewed. Sufficient redundancy should be planned for in information processing facilities.

Compliance: All statutory, regulatory, and contractual requirements for InfoSec and intellectual property should be documented, along with the methods for complying with each. Business records should be protected. Privacy and protection of PII should be ensured as required by applicable legislation, as well as any legal requirements for encryption. There should be regular independent reviews of InfoSec, business unit review of processes and procedures against policies and standards, and technical reviews of organizational information systems against its policies and standards.

ISO has also published a code of practice[3] based on these control categories for data controllers responsible for PII (personal data). In

---

3 ISO/IEC 29151:2017, Information technology — Security Techniques — Code of practice for personally identifiable information protection (Aug. 2017).

addition, it has extended the control set by adding these privacy controls based on the privacy principles of ISO 29000:[4] general policies for the use and protection of PII; consent and choice; purpose legitimacy and specification; collection limitation; data minimization; use, retention, and disclosure limitation; accuracy and quality; openness, transparency, and notice; individual participation and access; accountability; information security; and privacy compliance.

DPOs should consider how these privacy controls may be used to provide compliance with GDPR statutory and other contractual data protection obligations of their controller or processor organizations. Comprehensively, undertaking an audit based on the ISO 27001 processes utilizing both the ISO 27002 and ISO 29151 controls may provide a good part of the evidence needed for the DPO to determine if their organization is in compliance with the GDPR.

5.1.2 NIST

5.1.2.1 Process

The three objectives of information security are confidentiality, integrity, and availability (CIA). These respectively mean to keep data from being disclosed or lost, to preserve it in the state it was provided with only approved modifications, and to ensure it is there to be accessed when needed. The purpose is to avoid unauthorized access, use, disclosure, disruption, modification, or destruction. A more complete definition is provided under FISMA[5] as follows:[6]

Confidentiality: "Preserving authorized restrictions on information access and disclosure, including means for protecting personal privacy and proprietary information…" A loss of *confidentiality* is the unauthorized disclosure of information.

Integrity: "Guarding against improper information modification or destruction, and includes ensuring information non-repudiation and authenticity…" A loss of *integrity* is the unauthorized modification or destruction of information.

---

4 ISO/IEC 29000:2011, Information technology — Security Techniques — Privacy framework (Dec. 2011).
5 Federal Information Security Management Act (FISMA), Pub L. 107–347 (Dec. 2002).
6 FIPS, Pub. 199, Standards for Security Categorization of Federal Information and Information Systems (Feb. 2004).

Availability: "Ensuring timely and reliable access to and use of information…" A loss of *availability* is the disruption of access to or use of information or an information system.

To implement these three objectives, organizations set up information risk management programs. With the U.S. government, the Risk Management Framework[7] uses a seven-step process integrated into the system development life cycle. The first step is to prepare the organization; the second is to categorize the system and its information as low, moderate, or high risk; the third and fourth are to select, tailor, and implement initial set of controls (described below); the fifth is to assess the implementation and effectiveness of the controls;[8] the sixth to authorize the system based on a determination of risk to the organization; and the seventh is to monitor the effectiveness of the controls.

5.1.2.2 Controls

The NIST SP 800-53 provides a catalog of controls[9] used in the certification of new information systems for the U.S. government, across the following 20 categories. The controls are classified as either common that applies across many or all information systems in any organization, system-specific, or hybrid. In addition to InfoSec controls, the control catalog also has privacy controls, which are "to manage the privacy risks associated with an organization's creation, collection, use, processing, storage, maintenance, dissemination, disclosure, or disposal of PII separate from security concerns." Previously presented separately, the privacy controls are now integrated into the catalog, and sometimes a control will be designated as a joint security and privacy control.

Due to the vast size of the control catalog, only a small number of the InfoSec controls not noted already in the ISO 27002 discussion or privacy controls are listed in describing these categories below:

- *Access control*: previous login notification; device lock; wireless access; data mining protection.

---

7 NIST, SP 800-37 r2 (draft), Risk Management Framework for Information Systems and Organizations (Sept. 2017).
8 NIST, SP 800-53A r4, Assessing Security and Privacy Controls in Federal Information Systems and Organizations (Dec. 2014).
9 NIST, SP 800-53 r5 (draft), Security and Privacy Controls for Information Systems and Organizations (Aug. 2017).

- *Awareness and training*: training records.
- *Audit and accountability*: audit events; response to audit processing failures; audit review, analysis, and reporting.
- *Assessment, authorization, and monitoring*: continuous monitoring; penetration testing.
- *Configuration management*: baseline configuration; least functionality; system component inventory.
- *Contingency planning*: alternative processing site; system recovery and reconstitution.
- *Identification and authentication*: multifactor authentication; single sign-on; device identification and authentication; authenticator management; identity proofing.
- *Individual participation*: policies; consent; redress; privacy notice; individual access.
- *Incident response*: incident response testing; incident response training; information spillage response.
- *Maintenance*: maintenance tools; timely maintenance.
- *Media protection*: media sanitization; media downgrading.
- *Privacy authorization*: authority to collect; purpose specification; information sharing with external parties.
- *Physical and environmental protection*: visitor access records; fire protection; temperature and humidity controls.
- *Planning*: security and privacy architectures; rules of behavior (e.g., social media).
- *Program management*: critical infrastructure plan; insider threat program; threat awareness program; inventory of PII, privacy reporting; supply chain risk management plan.
- *Personnel security*: access agreements; external personnel security.
- *Risk assessment*: vulnerability scanning; criticality analysis.

- *System and services acquisition*: system development life cycle; external system services; developer testing and evaluation; component authenticity.

- *System and communications protection*: denial-of-service protection; application partitioning; boundary protection; PKI certificates; session authenticity; process isolation.

- *System and information integrity*: flaw remediation; system monitoring; software, firmware, and information integrity; information input validation; de-identification; data quality operations; limiting PII used in testing and dissemination.

DPOs should become familiar with the list of controls in the NIST control catalog, as these are more detailed than those in the ISO control catalog and should be an invaluable checklist to use when auditing InfoSec and privacy compliance. To audit the InfoSec requirements of Article 32, the DPO could utilize the ISO 27001 process and the ISO 27002 and NIST SP 800-53 catalogs of controls to ensure all necessary controls have been included and are operating effectively. To further extend that to privacy controls, the ISO 29151 controls and the NIST privacy controls could be added. In either case, the DPO would have had to first have audited the risk management processes of assessment and treatment for the organization's systems as a whole and any DPIAs performed for new technologies or processing, as described in Chapter 4.

5.1.3 Anonymization

One security technique that is mentioned in the GDPR is the use of anonymization. When data is made anonymous, it falls outside the GDPR, as Recital 26 states: "The principles of data protection should therefore not apply to anonymous information, namely information which does not relate to an identified or identifiable natural person or to personal data rendered anonymous in such a manner that the data subject is not or no longer identifiable. This Regulation does not therefore concern the processing of such anonymous information." The process of anonymization of personal data itself is a form of further processing requiring a legal basis, such as the legitimate interest of the controller. The methods used to anonymize personal data and their effectiveness is something a DPO should understand to be able to assess.

The WP29 opined on various methods of anonymization,[10] which should be required to be make re-identification of the personal data reasonably impossible. The controller should look first at the cost and the knowledge needed to use specific means to reverse the anonymization process, determining the severity and likelihood of such actions. This assessment must be done against the realization of increasing computing power and increasing availability of public datasets increases the re-identification risk over time and the risks of incomplete anonymization to cause harm to data subjects.

Also, event-level data that is handed over to a third-party by the controller, even though the events may be anonymized, are still considered personal data unless the data is aggregated before transfer to remove the individual events and the original dataset used by the controller is destroyed. An anonymized dataset must ensure that an individual cannot be identified and that individual records cannot be linked with the dataset. "Generally speaking, therefore, removing directly identifying elements in itself is not enough to ensure that identification of the data subject is no longer possible."

When anonymizing personal data, controllers need to be aware of the three risks to anonymized data: singling out records that identify an individual, linkability of records concerning the same data subject or group of data subjects, and inference of the value of an attribute for a set of other attributes. While no technique fully addresses all these risks all the time, two groups of anonymization techniques have been developed: generalization and randomization.

Randomization methods include: noise addition (to make the attributes less accurate); permutation (swapping attributes between records); and differential privacy (noise is added to each record upon a query, as the whole dataset is not released). Generalization dilutes the dataset's attributes and the methods include: aggregation and k-identity (city of resident to country or birthdate or salary specifics to ranges) and l-diversity/t-closeness (each attribute has at least l different values and at same distribution as originally).

Recommendations for anonymization include to not release and forget but to identify new threats that may impact the residual risk of re-identification; understand re-identification risk from non-anonymized parts of a dataset and correlations between attributes; consider

---

10 Art. 29 DP WP, Op. 5/2014 on Anonymisaton Techniques (Apr. 2014).

contextual elements, such as nature of the data, sample size, safeguards, how widely will data be released, publicly available data, and how attractive this data is to attackers; and consider technical elements, like removing unique attributes, disclosing the anonymization technique, and special considerations based on the anonymization technique used.

The DPO, in assessing the anonymization process to determine compliance with GDPR, must understand the difference between encryption, anonymization, and pseudonymization in that encrypted personal data and pseudonymized personal data still fall under the GDPR, as they can and are intended to be re-identified through the proper application of the encryption keys or linking data. Anonymized data cannot and is not intended to be re-identified, so is outside the GDPR but only if the personal data is completely anonymized. With that understanding, the DPO should focus on assessing whether the controller has followed the recommendations above, has identified the risks with each anonymization technique used, implemented appropriate treatments for those risks, and developed a life cycle process for anonymized personal data to keep track of it, all recipients, and new threats, data availability, and technologies increasing re-identification risk.

5.2 Data Breach and Privacy by Design

Articles 33 and 34 require the notification of the personal data breaches, as discussed in Chapter 3. A processor is to notify the controller and the controller notify the DPA unless it is unlikely to result in a risk to the rights and freedoms of data subjects and data subjects if there is a high risk. The controller must inform the DPA of the number and categories of data subjects and personal data records affected, measures taken to respond to the breach and mitigate its adverse effects, and the likely consequences. So, a DPO has several areas to understand in assessing the status of breach response: what types of security events are included in the definition of a breach; the processes and technologies used to identify, stop, and respond to a breach; how the level of risk for the notification threshold is determined; and the processes to gather data and then report to DPAs and data subjects as necessary.

Article 25 specifies the use of privacy by design (PbD) and default, which requires a deeper understanding of what those terms mean and examples of using these techniques. A DPO must be able to advise developers and system designers on proper PbD design consideration and then be able to review various types of privacy-enhancing technologies (PETs) that implement those designs.

5.2.1 Data Breach

5.2.1.1 Defining a Breach

Article 4(12) defines a personal data breach to mean "a breach of security leading to the accidental or unlawful destruction, loss, alteration, unauthorised disclosure of, or access to, personal data transmitted, stored or otherwise processed." The WP29 has stated that "whilst all personal data breaches are security incidents, not all security incidents are necessarily personal data breaches."[11] The WP29 categorizes types of personal data breaches as being ones impacting the InfoSec principles of confidentiality, integrity, and availability. Availability breaches may only be temporary, and controllers would have to consider whether the breach involves one of the other two InfoSec principles or impacts the rights and freedoms of data subjects.

While the breach notification requirements focus on the effects on personal data and the data subjects, defining what a breach is may be more difficult. The concept of a breach of an organization's data seems an easy one, but it is not always easy in agreeing on just what qualifies as a data breach. Is it only an attempt at unauthorized access to a system, or is it only the successful use of data acquired in an authorized manner to enrich the taker or harm the data subject? ENISA previously documented the differences of belief among EU data protection regulators about just what constitutes a data breach, while at the same time listing some types of breaches that organizations can refer to:[12]

- *Loss of IT equipment*: misplaced or stolen equipment — laptops, USB sticks, etcetera.

- *Mailing*: distribution of a letter in the mail or an email to an incorrect address that includes personal data.

---

11 Art. 29 DP WP, Guidelines on Personal data breach notification under Regulation 2016/679, r1 (Feb. 2018).
12 ENISA, Data breach notifications in the EU (Jan. 2011).

- *Improper disposal of documents*: leaving personal data in documents deposited in a garbage bin that can be accessed by the public.
- *Hacking*: malicious attacks on computer networks.
- *Technical error*: unforeseen complication in an IT system exposing data to outside parties.
- *Theft*: data in the form of documents, electronically stored data, etcetera that is stolen.
- *Unauthorized access*: employees taking advantage of vulnerabilities to access personal data of customers stored in files or electronically.
- *Unauthorized distribution*: distributing personal data on P2P networks.

The first important step for the DPO is to review what incidents or events that the organization has defined as being considered a breach. While there will likely be quite many security incidents that occur, it is only when there is an incident or event that fits within the organization's definition of a personal data breach that the full breach response notification process is then invoked. It also must be clear who in the controller's organization has the responsibility to declare an incident or event to be a breach, so that the breach response process can be initiated. A breach may not involve personal data, so the organization must know how to differentiate.

5.2.1.2 Breach Response

In the typical non-outsourced data environment, the organization must undertake many steps to prepare for and respond to data breaches. This assumes the implementation of a rigorous information security and privacy program as explained above and that there is a defined incident response program with various detection, correction, and recovery capabilities and that the steps in the program are regularly tested and re-validated after each incident. The following steps that focus just on the data breach program include:

- Define exactly what is and what is not considered a data breach (e.g., is any unauthorized access a data breach?) and when it is a breach of personal data.

- Determine which specific information is considered to be in-scope personal data and understand whether it is encrypted and when (at rest, in transit, in use).
- Have a complete map to where all data is currently located and how each is classified.
- Understand the automated incident detection tools, including from IDSes, malware detectors, logging analyzers, etcetera.
- Have list of security incident types and methods to quantify the severity levels, including those effecting personal data.
- Understand the exact security incident level triggers that start the data breach process and who makes the decision it is a breach.
- Create an incident response team, with members from all applicable disciplines, including information security, legal, data owners, public relations, and top executives.
- Make a breach response contact list and an escalation personnel list.
- Define the breach response steps (e.g., analysis, quarantine, contain, eradicate, gather evidence, recover, investigate, review), and create a priority for the steps, including what causes escalation to each succeeding level.
- Define the technical processes that would be used to quarantine various types of intrusions, repair the infected systems, restore affected data, and determine and apply remediations to prevent recurrence.
- Understand which breach notification statutes apply and the organization's responsibilities under each (e.g., GDPR, ePrivacy Directive, other countries' data breach laws).
- Determine the role that law enforcement will play and the applicable law enforcement agencies.
- Determine if there are contractual requirements with the organization's customers or vendors to notify them in case of a data breach.

- Understand the notification process involving applicable regulatory officials, such as DPAs and others.

- Prepare the respective breach response roles for public relations (for business reputation and brand impacts), customer relationship management, and help desk support (to deal with consumer calls).

- Train on, monitor, and keep up to date the intrusion detection and prevention tools and processes.

- Create a process for legal review after a breach to determine potential legal liabilities and litigation strategies.

- Prepare for the possibilities of implementing consumer credit monitoring and identify theft prevention efforts.

- Understand all the potential costs of a data breach and which of these are covered by insurance.

- Regularly review all security and intrusion incidents, even if they do not lead to a breach and document and implement all remediation actions.

- Test run a practice intrusion leading to breach with the appropriate members of the incident response team.

In the outsourced environment, such as that of cloud computing, planning for and responding to data breaches has several new aspects.[13] Each of these new aspects introduces a potential risk, and, as such, the organization needs to adapt an appropriate risk treatment for each. All coordination activities will need to occur between the organization and the primary cloud service provider (CSP), and, if several are involved, the primary CSP needs to ensure that the secondary CSPs have synchronized their data breach response procedures appropriately.

- *The CSP will now be the first to know when a breach occurs.* The CSP, through its own monitoring and incident detection capabilities, will likely be the first to know that a breach has occurred. This means that the incident response procedures of the CSP will be invoked, including the determination if

---

13 See Thomas J. Shaw, *Legal Response to Data Breaches in the Cloud* (in the Appendix).

there has been a breach. But as the organization retains the legal obligations and exposures after a breach, it must be fully involved in these determinations. As such, the incident response procedures, including the determination of whether a breach has occurred, must fully involve the organization. It must not only integrate its procedures for incident response and escalation with the CSP's procedures but must ensure that it maintains an accurate and up-to-date contact list with CSP, including holiday contact information.

- *The multitenant environment may make it more difficult to determine who is affected.* The rigorous isolation controls in the multitenant environment ensure that the co-tenants are always kept virtually segregated. But as attacks may be against physical and not logical devices and environments, and, as such, it may not be easy to tell which tenants are affected by a breach. This complexity in the multitenant environment can be addressed by having monitoring tools imbedded inside the virtualization system, to help identify unauthorized activity and the affected areas and tenants. There may be monitoring and investigation tools that can be extended from the CSP to the customer to assist with the organization's own breach response activities.

- *The definition of a breach may be different.* The various CSPs will have differing definitions of what they consider a data breach. Some may consider a breach to only occur if there is a violation of the local applicable laws, while others may require proof that data has been removed and utilized in a manner harmful to the data subjects. Organizations would most likely want to know of any unauthorized access to their systems and data and then be able to determine how to comply with their applicable statutory, regulatory, and contractual obligations. The organization and the CSP need to ensure they have come to a complete agreement about this definition.

- *The conflicting breach notification statutes.* The proliferating number of such statutes and regulatory rules may make it extremely complex for a CSP to respond completely to all these requirements. Besides, it may be not clear whether the CSP or the organization is always primarily responsible for responding to the breach notification requirements. The organization must clarify the respective roles of the organization and the CSP in the case of a breach in each applicable jurisdiction. Sending breach notification notices may be more logical for the CSP to do, but it may want to be compensated accordingly if it is not at fault for the breach.

- *If and to which law enforcement body to report to.* If the data breach impacts more than a single state or country, there will be differing law enforcement agencies to report to and get involved. Again, the CSP and the organization need to determine the roles of each in reporting to the appropriate law enforcement agencies and under which circumstances a report should be made. For their own differing business reasons, the organization and the CSP may or may not want to report a breach to law enforcement.

- *The differing RPOs and RTOs of customers may complicate a breach-related recovery.* The organization will have a specific minimum amount of data loss (RPO — Recovery Point Objective) and maximum recovery time (RTO — Recovery Time Objective) that it will accept if the breach affects data such that it requires a recovery. Multiple tenant environments will likely have to move to both the minimum RTO and maximum RPO to satisfy all the tenants. Organizations will want to find a way to have their business continuity requirements appropriately addressed.

- *The impacts of different cloud service models.* Software as a Service customers have the least control and so may have to rely totally on the breach response processes and capabilities of the CSP. Platform as a Service customers may have additional visibility and control, and Infrastructure as a Service even more so over the breach response, recovery, and investigation procedures. So, organizations will need to consider the multiple cloud service models that they use and have multiple breach response procedures utilizing the tools that are available with each. This will also likely impact the RTOs and RPOs that are obtainable.

- *Differing rules of escalation, quarantine, and remediation.* The CSP and the organization will have different rules for when to escalate the data breach, to quarantine the source of the data breach and remediate the problem. When the organization has less leverage with the CSP, it may need to use its own procedures to create a superset of breach response procedures. When is has more leverage, it will need to integrate each of these areas to the fullest extent possible, but even then, there will be some differences, as the CSP has a wider audience it must address, so the organization should also maintain a superset of rules for breach response.

- *Reduced visibility to problem.* The tools that organizations use to understand breaches, such as intrusion detection alerts and system and transaction logs, may not be available. Physical access to servers for forensic analysis or to unplug the network, to hit the reset button or to reboot systems if all else fails, is not available either. The usual admin access levels may not be available, as those may be retained by the CSP. Network connections may also be affected. To address some of this, a secure channel (VPN) connection to the organization's systems to analyze problems and communicate is needed, as well as network or application monitoring capabilities, and some forensic analysis and collection of alerts and logs.

- *Difficulty in fully testing the breach response procedures.* As with an incident response process, from the smallest misconfiguration to a full-blown disaster, it is vital to go beyond the paper design and actually test the procedures under at least a mock incident occurrence scenario. This is the only way to understand how well the procedures will work and how well the various participants understand their roles. With a data breach when the data in hosted by a CSP, this may not be easy to do. For data under the SaaS model, the CSP may be resource-constrained to be able to participate in each customer's data breach response exercises. For data under the IaaS model, the CSP may not feel any obligation to do so, assuming they have made reasonable efforts to provide appropriate security in the areas for which they remain responsible. As such, the organization may have to perform such exercises which a surrogate acting for the CSP, hopefully based on their incident response procedures.

Organizations must not only risk assess CSPs and integrate its data breach handling procedures with those of the CSP, but also should do the same with any of its business partners with whom it shares its confidential data and then regularly update these risk assessments to ensure that its security safeguards and those of its partners continue to be rigorous and the likelihood of a breach is minimized to the extent possible.

5.2.1.3 Determining Breach Severity

ENISA, as part of the data breach response requirements under the ePrivacy Directive, published technical guidelines[14] that recommend a process based on ISO 27035 for information security incidents with the following five phases: plan and prepare; detect and assess; notify and respond; collect evidence and forensics; and review and improve. Some of the guidelines are specific to that legislation, but most are generally application to the GDPR.

The first phase includes implementing a risk management framework like that described in Chapter 4 and risk treatments controls as described in the previous section above. A few important controls include documenting anyone who comes into contract with personal data, access controls over personal data, where encryption is used, encryption algorithms and key management, secure deletion techniques, and system and event logging. The breach response must also be created and tested.

The second phase starts with notification of the breach by technical or human means, triggering an assessment. ENISA recommends two levels of assessment: the initial assessment intending to be completed to be able to respond within the statutory periods and a later more detailed assessment. The initial assessment would need to determine the cause of the event; the people and data records affected; an estimate of the severity of the breach by looking at the data; its ability to identify an individual (more personal data elements increase identifiability); and the

---

14 ENISA, Recommendations on technical implementation guidelines (Apr. 2012).

level of the exposure based on type of exposure, preventative controls, and delay in reporting; and any immediate response measures to take. Charting the identifiability against the exposure level leads to rating the impact as low, medium, high, or very high.

The third phase requires taking immediate and later containment response measures, such as changing or removing authentication credentials, keys, system or network access, new software processes or files, devices, storage locations, and limiting access to attacked services or entry points. It is also here that DPAs or data subjects would be notified. The fourth phase starts from first awareness of the breach by gathering evidence, following appropriate chain of custody procedures by preserving evidence needed for law enforcement and later forensic analysis. The fifth phase includes lessons learned to improve the InfoSec controls and the breach response process.

ENISA later formalized its methodology for severity of personal data breaches.[15] The severity is the magnitude of the potential impact on individuals from the breach. The three elements used are the type of personal data breached in context, ease of identification of the individual from the data breached, and the circumstances of the breach. The criticality of the data used (simple, behavioral, financial, or sensitive) in the processing context (volume of data breached, vulnerability of data subjects, publicly available, etcetera) is reduced if identification is difficult (negligible, limited, significant, or maximum) but increased by specific circumstances (loss of confidentiality, integrity, accessibility, or malicious intent).

The DPO must step through each phase of the data breach response program and determine whether the controller or processor has completed each activity. If the controller or processor is part of a cloud or other shared environment, determine whether these additional considerations have been addressed. The DPO should understand the breach response process in both the procedural/technical aspects and the legal/breach notification aspects and ensure that those obligations work together seamlessly. This especially arises in evaluating the design and testing of the breach severity assessment procedures to determine whether notification is mandatory.

---

15 ENISA, Recommendations for a methodology of the assessment of severity of personal data breaches (Dec. 2013).

5.2.2 Privacy by Design and Default

5.2.2.1 Requirements and Principles

Under Article 25, controllers are required to implement effective technical and organizational measures that are designed with data protection principles in mind. This is termed privacy by design (PbD). The controller needs to do this both when determining the means of processing and during the actual processing. This means adding data protection measures into the processing needs to begin from the earliest stages of the product or service life cycle. Pseudonymization is mentioned as one technique to accomplish PbD. This requires according to Recital 29 that the information linking personal data to the data subject be kept security and separately to protect against unauthorized reversals of pseudonymized data. Along with that is the requirement that by default the minimum amount (necessary for that purpose) of personal data is processed, with the minimum amount of processing done, including retention of the data and accessibility of the data to others without consent.

The concept of PbD originated with the IPC of the Canadian province of Ontario and is based upon seven foundational principles:[16]

- *Proactive* not Reactive; *Preventative* not Remedial:
  The PbD approach is characterized by proactive rather than reactive measures. It anticipates and prevents privacy invasive events before they happen. PbD does not wait for privacy risks to materialize, nor does it offer remedies for resolving privacy infractions once they have occurred — it aims to prevent them from occurring. In short, PbD comes before the fact, not after.

- Privacy as the *Default Setting*:
  We can all be certain of one thing: The default rules! PbD seeks to deliver the maximum degree of privacy by ensuring that personal data is automatically protected in any given IT system or business practice. If an individual does nothing, their privacy still remains intact. No action is required on the part of the individual to protect their privacy — it is built into the system, by default.

---

16 Ontario IPC, Privacy by Design (rev. Sept. 2013).

- Privacy *Embedded* into Design:
  PbD is embedded into the design and architecture of IT systems and business practices. It is not bolted on as an add-on after the fact. The result is that privacy becomes an essential component of the core functionality being delivered. Privacy is integral to the system, without diminishing functionality.

- Full Functionality — *Positive-Sum*, not Zero-Sum:
  PbD seeks to accommodate all legitimate interests and objectives in a positive-sum win-win manner, not through a dated, zero-sum approach, where unnecessary trade-offs are made. PbD avoids the pretense of false dichotomies, such as privacy versus security — demonstrating that it is possible to have.

- End-to-End Security — *Full Lifecycle Protection*:
  PbD, having been embedded into the system prior to the first element of information being collected, extends securely throughout the entire life cycle of the data involved — strong security measures are essential to privacy, from start to finish. This ensures that all data is securely retained, then securely destroyed at the end of the process in a timely fashion. Thus, PbD ensures cradle-to-grave, secure life cycle management of information, end to end.

- *Visibility* and *Transparency* — Keep it *Open*:
  PbD seeks to assure all stakeholders that whatever the business practice or technology involved, it is, in fact, operating according to the stated promises and objectives, subject to independent verification. Its component parts and operations remain visible and transparent to users and providers alike. Remember, trust but verify.

- *Respect* for User Privacy — Keep it *User Centric*:
  Above all, PbD requires architects and operators to protect the interests of the individual by offering such measures as strong privacy defaults, appropriate notice, and empowering user-friendly options. Keep it user centric.

5.2.2.2 Privacy by Design Applied

While the GDPR requirements target controller organizations, Recital 78 encourages the producers of products, services, and applications to also implement the PbD principles, which, in turn, makes it easier for controllers and processors to meet their DP obligations. A DPO needing to advise a controller organization on PbD should first gain an understanding of the many aspects of PbD, such as how it applies to privacy engineering, how it has been applied by organizations, how it is applied to specific technologies, and how privacy and security can both be implemented by design.

Privacy engineering is a means of including privacy as a non-functional requirement when new processing or technologies are introduced or revised. After performing a risk assessment, the privacy controls need to be selected. A paper[17] from the IPC suggests that there are two approaches, Privacy by policy ("trust us") and Privacy by architecture ("trust the system"). The former is the typical approach used today, although addressing privacy risk is not always fully embedded into the systems development life cycle. The latter depends on either data minimization or moving the data closer to control by the data subject.

Data minimization would be an architectural choice not to collect and process data. An example described was that a company wanted to hire a job candidate in a certain salary range, but the candidate did not want to lose leverage and provide that information, either to the organization or the external HR recruiter. Instead, the recruiter provided a random number to the organization, which added it to the top of its salary range and passed the resulting number to the candidate. The candidate subtracted their salary and passed the resulting number to the recruiter, who compared it to the original random number. If it was lower than the original number, the candidate would fit within the salary range. Importantly from the privacy perspective, the personal salary data never came under the control of either the organization or the recruiter.

If architectural design does not sufficiently reduce residual risk, then the technical controls of the kind discussed in the first section are appropriate. These include the access controls, authentication, logging, and intrusion detection systems. Obfuscation includes using encryption

---

17 Ontario IPC, Privacy Engineering: Proactively Embedding Privacy, by Design (Jan. 2014).

and pseudonymization, where data is replaced by codes stored elsewhere. And data minimization prevents storage of all but necessary personal data.

Combining PbD with security leads to the seven foundational principals of security by design.[18] Important ideas here are the InfoSec can be deployed to enable, as well as protect organizations, that InfoSec should be for both the enterprise and individual stakeholders, InfoSec should be embedded into hardware and software, end-to-end security, and that there should be security by default. This concept implies that the use of least privilege (minimum authorizations and resources necessary), need-to-know (information), least trust (of system components), mandatory access controls, and segregation of duties.

As an enterprise, IBM[19] implemented a PbD program that focused on three areas: PIAs, training and awareness in privacy, and data incident management. The PIAs use a web tool for a self-assessment where the business process or application owner can immediately view the privacy risks flagged. A customized knowledgebase provides actions items that can address the privacy risks and track them to resolution. The online training reinforces privacy messages into simple knowledge nuggets with a takeaway message reinforced by placing it in the context of real-world situations. A data incident tool is used globally to log all incidents and guide the incident owner through a standardized process of incident response and follow through. In total, these PbD processes allow for building standardized processes that have minimized the collection and use of personal data.

There is a variety of technologies that PbD has been applied to, including big data, biometrics, mobile devices, smart meters and smart grids, health information, digital marketing, and geolocation. The following PbD features embedded in a big data sense-making system (used to allow organizations to make decisions of all the data that they have but do not have current insights into):[20]

- "Full Attribution: Every observation (record) needs to know from where it came and when. There cannot be merge/purge

---

18 Ontario IPC, Privacy and Security by Design: An Enterprise Architecture Approach (Sept. 2013).
19 Ontario IPC, Privacy by Design: From Policy to Practice (Sept. 2011).
20 Ontario IPC, Privacy by Design: In the Age of Big Data (June 2012).

data survivorship processing whereby some observations or fields are discarded.

- Data Tethering: Adds, changes and deletes occurring in systems of record must be accounted for, in real time, in sub-seconds.

- Analytics on Anonymized Data: The ability to perform advanced analytics over cryptographically altered data means organizations can anonymize more data before information sharing.

- Tamper-Resistant Audit Logs: Every user search should be logged in a tamper-resistant manner — even the database administrator should not be able to alter the evidence contained in this audit log.

- False Negative Favoring Methods: The capability to more strongly favor false negatives is of critical importance in systems that could be used to affect someone's civil liberties.

- Self-Correcting False Positives: With every new data point presented, prior assertions are re-evaluated to ensure they are still correct, and if no longer correct, these earlier assertions can often be repaired — in real time.

- Information Transfer Accounting: Every secondary transfer of data, whether to human eyeball or a tertiary system, can be recorded to allow stakeholders (e.g., data custodians or the consumers themselves) to understand how their data is flowing."

For app developers on mobile devices, PbD practices recommend[21] following global privacy practices at a minimum for personal data accessed by an app, such as collection limitation and data minimization, employ notice and informed consent, utilize appropriate security practices, use privacy by default settings, ensure end-to-end protection of data, and include privacy as a core functionality in the app. In general, software developers must deal with three aspects of security by design: "i) software security assurance (designing software systems that are secure from the ground up and minimizing the impact of system breach when a security

---

21 Ontario IPC, The Roadmap for Privacy by Design in Mobile Communications: A Practical Tool for Developers, Service Providers, and Users (Dec. 2010).

vulnerability is discovered); ii) preserving privacy in the enterprise environment and; iii) ensuring identity across heterogeneous vendors."[22]

An organization implementing PbD should ensure that the PbD processes and practices:[23]

- "Apply to the design and architecture of infrastructure, IT systems, practices that interact with or involve the use of any personal information.

- Describe each of the core purposes served and main functions delivered by those infrastructures, systems and practices, including but not limited to the provision of security and the protection of privacy in personal information.

- Incorporate data minimization and provide the highest degree of privacy protection for personal information possible while serving the other core purposes and delivering the other main functions.

- Provide this degree of privacy protection by employing the maximum feasible means needed to ensure the security, confidentiality, and integrity of personal information throughout the life cycle of the data, from its original collection, through to its use, storage, dissemination, and secure destruction at the end of the life cycle.

- Whenever reasonably possible, provide for that privacy protection automatically, so that no action is required for individual users or customers to protect the privacy of their personal information.

- Ensure that infrastructure, IT systems, and business practices that interact with or involve the use of any personal information remain reasonably transparent and subject to independent verification by all relevant stakeholders, including customers, users, and affiliated organizations.

- Emphasize the design and maintenance of user-centric systems and practices, including strong privacy defaults, appropriate notice, and other user-friendly options."

---

22 Ontario IPC, Privacy and Security by Design: A Convergence of Paradigms (Jan. 2013).

23 Ontario IPC, Privacy by Design in Law, Policy and Practice: A White Paper for Regulators, Decision-makers and Policy-makers (Aug. 2011).

To support PbD, organizations need to provide appropriate privacy and InfoSec training, track all projects dealing with systems that involve processing of personal data, require privacy design documents for all projects from the start, and have the privacy design documents reviewed by management and audited by the internal audit team.

ENISA has looked at how to implement PbD, moving from the legal obligations to the technologies designed and then implemented.[24] These technologies are termed privacy enhancing technologies (PETs), and some common implementations include encryption in providing secure private communications, anonymous and pseudonymous communications protocols, attribute-based credentials, authentication (separated from identity proofing), privacy-preserving data mining, storage privacy, privacy-preserving computations, and private searches of database, along with technologies that enhance transparency and intervenability (for data subject rights).

To implement PETs, the use of PbD must consider different possible strategies at the design phase. Eight of these strategies are:[25]

Minimize	The amount of personal data should be restricted to the minimal amount possible (data minimization).
Hide	Personal data and their interrelations should be hidden from plain view.
Separate	Personal data should be processed in a distributed fashion, in separate compartments whenever possible.
Aggregate	Personal data should be processed at the highest level of aggregation and with the least possible detail in which it is (still) useful.
Inform	Data subjects should be adequately informed whenever processed (transparency).
Control	Data subjects should be provided agency over the processing of their personal data.
Enforce	A privacy policy compatible with legal requirements should be in place and should be enforced.
Demonstrate	Data controllers must be able to demonstrate compliance with privacy policy into force and any applicable legal requirements.

---

24 ENISA, Privacy and Data Protection by Design — from policy to engineering (Dec. 2014).
25 ENISA, Privacy by design in big data — An overview of privacy enhancing technologies in the era of big data analytics (Dec. 2015).

ENISA looked at how PbD could operate in tandem with big data. The basic principles of two seem to be in conflict. In big data, to identify trends and detect patterns, the largest dataset possible is preferred, in opposition to the data minimization and limited data retention principles. Repurposing of data for further processing is contrary to the notice and consent principles. The PbD principles were applied to each big data phase to address the issues: data acquisition/collection (minimize, aggregate, hide, notice, control); data analysis and creation (aggregate, hide); data storage (hide, separate); data usage (aggregate); and all phases (enforce, demonstrate).

ENISA has also developed an assessment methodology to determine if PETs are sufficiently mature,[26] evaluated web portals for PETs,[27] proposed a PETs maturity repository for general use,[28] and PETs control matrix for online and mobile users.[29] This latter tool considers PETs under general assessment criteria of maturity and stability, privacy policy implementation, and usability and specific assessment criteria of secure messaging, VPNs, anonymizing networks, and anti-tracking tools for online browsing.

The Office of the Privacy Commissioner (OPC) of Canada published a report on PETs.[30] The scope of this report was PETs applying to data in transit (as opposed to in storage). Instead of categorizing PETs by technology as ENISA does, OPC categorizes them by the capabilities provided to end users. The categories are: informed consent (e.g., using data tagging with a sticky machine reading privacy always attached to the data); data minimization (e.g., digital footprint privacy erasers and private browsing); data tracking (e.g., dashboard of prior data disclosures); anonymity (e.g., communications anonymizers, such as TOR); control (e.g., attribute-based credentials and self-sovereign identity); negotiate terms and conditions (users set the terms of the

---

26 ENISA, Readiness Analysis for the Adoption and Evolution of Privacy Enhancing Technologies Methodology, Pilot Assessment, and Continuity Plan (Dec. 2015).
27 ENISA, Online privacy tools for the general public — Towards a methodology for the evaluation of PETs for internet & mobile users (Dec. 2015).
28 ENISA, Privacy Enhancing Technologies: Evolution and State of the Art — A Community Approach to PETs Maturity Assessment (Dec. 2016).
29 ENISA, PETs controls matrix — A systematic approach for assessing online and mobile privacy tools (Dec. 2016).
30 OPC, Privacy Enhancing Technologies — A Review of Tools and Techniques (Nov. 2017).

privacy they are willing to accept, such as the Platform for Privacy Preferences Project); technical enforcement (e.g., using software to ensure negotiated privacy terms are actually being carried out instead of merely promised with endpoint event detection and web transparency tools); remote audit of enforcement (e.g., trust marks); and use of legal rights (e.g., automated tools to exercise data subject rights, such as those under the GDPR).

The DPO monitoring GDPR compliance is required to be involved with all DP issues and should be involved at the earliest stages of new systems, applications, technologies, and business processes. There are a variety of measures that can be applied generally to implement PbD at these early stages, including DPIAs, training and awareness, all InfoSec controls discussed above, anonymization, pseudonymization, privacy by architecture, and data minimization. More specifically, PbD must be understood at the design phase of systems by assessing the proper PbD design strategy to use to address the privacy risks. Then, that design strategy should be implemented using an appropriate PETs, which should be evaluated against ENISA maturity levels and control matrices as available and considering the end user capability provided as per the OPC.

The DPO should encourage their organization to take a proactive, enterprise-level approach to implementing PbD as a policy and process, following the steps identified above. The DPO could also consider the IAPP's Strategic PbD process for further insights. Regardless of the methodology used, any PbD solution must be evaluated by returning to the Article 25 requirements, that it be based on what is currently possible with technology, its cost of implementation and operation, and the likelihood and severity of risks to the rights and freedoms of data subjects, along with the nature, scope, context, and purposes of the processing.

CHAPTER 6

DPO Tasks — Outside the EU

There are several situations when the DPO must think beyond just EU geography, law, and culture. The first is when the controller or processor is involved in transferring personal data from within the EEA to a location outside the EEA. This requires the DPO to understand in detail one of the five complex mechanisms available to transfer personal data outside the region. The second is when the controller or processor themselves are not located within the EU and the impact on the DPO's role and its interplay with the role of the EU representative. The third is when the DPO themselves are not located within the EU. The fourth is dealing with non-EU data protection laws.

The movement of the personal data of EU residents has been the focus on many court challenges and supervisory actions very recently. The revelations regarding the activities of surveillance agencies led to court cases on the personal data transfer mechanism between the EU and the U.S. and the standard contractual clauses commonly used between companies. Because these cases are interesting for legal reasons but not within the scope of the DPO's tasks, they are not discussed here but are covered in the companion book.[1] Instead, this chapter looks at the data transfer mechanisms as specified by the GDPR and non-EU controllers, processors, DPOs, and privacy laws.

---

1 Thomas J. Shaw, *Information and Internet Law — Global Practice*, Ch. 3.

> **DPO Areas of Focus**
> - Transferring personal data outside the EU
> - Controllers and processors not present in the EU
> - DPO roles stationed outside the EU
> - Privacy laws in other countries and regions

6.1 Transferring Data Outside the EU

There are only four principal methods under which transfers of personal data outside the European Economic Areas (EEA) are legal. The EEA is made up of the 28 EU member states and Iceland, Norway, and Lichtenstein, the latter three of which have also committed to enacting the GDPR. A controller or processor not utilizing one of these methods would be violating Article 44 and be subject to administrative fines. So, it is important for the DPO to fully understand how each of these methods works, as there are strict requirements to be able to determine that the controller or processor is compliant with the GDPR.

6.1.1 Adequacy and Derogations

6.1.1.1 Adequacy

Countries that have been determined to have an adequate data protection regime comparable to that of the EU can be qualified by an adequacy decision of the EC. Under Article 45, so-called third countries, those outside the EU that have not adopted the GDPR, territories, or sectors within those third countries or international organizations (e.g., United Nations) can have personal data transferred to them without specific authorization if their data protection regime has been determined to be adequate. Recital 104 defines this as offering "guarantees ensuring an adequate level of protection essentially equivalent to that ensured" in the EU. This includes the data protection principles and data subject rights, along with procedural and enforcement mechanisms.[2]

---

2 Art. 29 DP WP, Adequacy Referential (Feb. 2018).

When making such an adequacy decision, the EC will inter alia consider the general rule of law and respect for human rights and freedoms in the country, its laws, and their implementation, including how public authorities have access to personal data, its data protection and security rules and case law, the enforcement of data subject rights and effectiveness of administrative and judicial redress for data subjects who personal data is transferred, an effective independent data protection supervisory authority, and the international data protection agreements the country has entered into and participation in related multilateral systems.

In one of its most recent adequacy decisions dealing with Uruguay,[3] the EC looked at the constitution of the country and its data protection laws to find a fundamental right to data protection. It found that the legal standards for protection of personal data in Uruguay were based upon those of the DPD, and the DP principles were found in the statute or explained by the supervisory authority. It found adequate judicial and administrative remedies for data subjects and that the supervisory authority was independent and had sufficient powers. It also noted that the country was a party to conventions on human rights and that it had ratified the Council of Europe's Convention for the Protection of Individuals with regard to Automatic Processing of Personal Data.[4]

Adequacy decisions made under the DPD will remain valid unless there is a change made to that decision. The EC will monitor decisions made under both the DPD and the GDPR, and decisions made under the GDPR will be subject to review every four years. If in its monitoring the EC determines that a third country no longer ensures adequate levels of data protection, it can repeal, amend, or suspend its prior adequacy decision. Such an action does not affect the other data transfer mechanisms under other articles.

There are currently 12 adequacy decisions involving Andorra, Argentina, Canada (for organizations subject to PIPEDA), Faeroe Islands, Guernsey, Isle of Man, Israel, Jersey, New Zealand, Switzerland, Uruguay, and the United States, with Japan and South Korea under

---

3 Commission Implementing Decision of 21 Aug. 2012 pursuant to Directive 95/46/EC of the European Parliament and of the Council on the adequate protection of personal data by the Eastern Republic of Uruguay with regard to automated process of personal data.

4 ETS No. 108 (Jan. 1981).

active consideration. The agreement with the U.S. has been subject to significant controversy and court cases, which are discussed in the companion book.[5]

The current mechanism for transfers of personal data from the EU to the United States is the EU-U.S. Privacy Shield, determined to be adequate by the EC in 2016.[6] The Privacy Shield requires organizations to self-certify that they adhere to the following privacy principles: notice, choice, accountability for onward transfers, security, data integrity and purpose limitation, access and recourse, enforcement, and liability, and that they have a publicly available privacy policy stating these commitments and other information. While self-certification is voluntary, once an organization joins the framework, these commitments become legal obligations.

Binding arbitration is one of the recourse mechanisms available to data subjects, and certified organizations commit to cooperating with EU DPAs in the investigation and resolution of complaints. The EC lists[7] five complaint channels: directly to the company, using an arbitration body, going through an EU DPA, going directly to the U.S. DPA (the FTC), or to the Privacy Shield Panel. The Privacy Shield ombudsman mechanism is a role set up independent of U.S. intelligence agencies that can handle complaints related to federal governmental agencies (public authorities) through an EU DPA. This role can deal with personal data issues involving public authorities transferred under the Privacy Shield, BCRs, or SCCs mechanisms.

6.1.1.2 Derogations

When one of the other transfer mechanisms is not available, controllers may be able to rely upon certain derogations to the prohibition on transfers outside the EEA. Under Article 49, personal data may be transferred based upon the explicit consent of the data subject, necessary for performance of a contract involving the data subject, important public interest reason based in EU law, legal claims or defenses, or the

---

5 Thomas J. Shaw, *Information and Internet Law — Global Practice*, Ch. 3.
6 Commission Implementing Decision (EU) 2016/1250 of 12 July 2016 pursuant to Directive 95/46/EC of the European Parliament and of the Council on the adequacy of the protection provided by the EU-U.S. Privacy Shield (notified under document C(2016) 4176).
7 EC, Guide to the EU-U.S. Privacy Shield (Aug. 2016).

vital interest of a data subject incapable of consenting. A compelling legitimate interest of the controller may also be a basis for transfer, subject to balancing against the interest, rights, and freedoms of the data subjects and fulfilling other requirements.

6.1.2 SCCs and BCRs

6.1.2.1 SCCs

Under Article 46, there are several types of contractual clauses for personal data transfers outside the EEA between unrelated entities. Controllers or processors may use standard contractual clauses (SCCs) adopted by the EC or the relevant DPA without requiring specific authorization from the DPA. SCCs have come under attack from DPAs.[8] Other contractual clauses between and among controllers, processors, and recipients do require specific authorization by the relevant DPA. Prior authorizations or decisions by DPAs or the EC under the DPD will remain in effect until revoked or amended.

There are two types of SCCs currently approved by the EC under the DPD. These are for transfers from an EU controller to a non-EEA controller and transfers from an EU controller to a non-EEA processor. The required elements in the controller ("data exporter") to controller ("data importer") agreement include[9] contact details; an explanation of the transfer, including categories of personal data and purposes for the transfer; third-party beneficiaries' clause, which allows data subjects to enforce the agreement; the obligations of both the data importer and data exporter; joint and several liability for both parties and indemnity for the non-violating party; the use of mediation or judicial remedies; cooperation with the DPAs and that the parties cannot vary the agreement. A later amendment provided a second set of clauses that allowed the addition of commercial clauses and for the ability of the DPA to suspend transfers.[10]

---

8 See Thomas J. Shaw, *EU data transfers to the U.S. — Model clauses but why?* (in the Appendix).
9 Commission Decision 2001/497/EC of 15 June 2001 on standard contractual clauses for the transfer of personal data to third countries, under Directive 95/46/EC.
10 Commission Decision 2004/915/EC of 27 Dec. 2004 amending Decision 2001/497/EC as regards the introduction of an alternative set of standard contractual clauses for the transfer of personal data to third countries.

It important for controllers who engage processors outside the EEA to understand that all their GDPR obligations cannot be presumed to be incorporated into the SCCs, despite their approval by the EC. For example, Article 28(3)(c) requires a commitment to confidentiality by processor personnel. Controllers must verify that their agreements with processors include all the duties and responsibilities required by the GDPR, including the specifics stated in the SCCs.

6.1.2.2 BCRs

Under Article 46, binding corporate rules (BCRs) are also authorized as a transfer mechanism. BCRs are described under Article 47, which will be approved by the relevant DPA is they bind all the members of the corporate group, including their employees, give data subjects clear enforceable rights related to the processing of their personal data, and specify at a minimum the following requirements. BCRs must describe:

- Structure and contact details for the group.
- The categories of personal data transferred, the processing type and purpose, the type of data subjects, and the third countries.
- The rules legally binding nature.
- The application of general data protection principles.
- The rights of data subjects and how they exercise those rights.
- Acceptance of liability by group member established in the EU for rule breaches by group members not established in the EU.
- Information on the rules is provided to data subjects.
- Tasks of DPO in monitoring rule compliance.
- Complaint procedures.
- Methods for ensuring compliance with the rules.
- How changes to rules are reported, including to DPAs.
- Cooperation mechanism with DPAs.
- How non-EU laws might impact guarantees in the rules.
- DP training.

The WP29 has revised the two sets of criteria to be used when submitting a BCR to a DPA for approval. These are for controllers inside the EU who transfer data outside the EU to a controller or processor within the same corporate group as the original controller (BCR-Controllers)[11] and for controllers inside the EU who transfer data outside the EU to a processor not in the same corporate group and the processing is done within that processor's corporate group (BCR-Processors).[12] The original controller and the original processor would be bound by a controller-processor agreement as would any subprocessors.

6.1.2.3 Judicial Transfers

Under Article 48, litigation-related demands by courts in non-EU countries for access to personal data within the EU must go through the process of mutual legal assistance treaties (MLATs). This point is an ongoing issue between U.S. courts that provide for generous rules of discovery of the opposing party's data and the rules of discovery in the EU, which are more restrictive. This matter is discussed further in the companion book.[13]

6.2 Non-EU Controllers and Privacy Laws

The DPO will encounter non-EU situations to address beyond just the transfer of personal data outside the EEA. These will occur when either the controller or processor is not located within the EU or when the DPO themselves are not located within the EU. Perhaps in coordination with being outside the EU but also for EU-based organizations, there is a strong likelihood the needs of international business will require dealing with non-EU laws, including privacy laws. The DPO needs to know how to respond in each of these non-EU situations, which is why global experience was a listed job skill in Chapter 1.

---

11 Art. 29 DP WP, Working Document setting up a table with the elements and principles to be found in binding corporate rules (updated) (Feb. 2018).
12 Art. 29 DP WP, Working Document setting up a table with the elements and principles to be found in Processor binding corporate rules (updated) (Feb. 2018).
13 Thomas J. Shaw, *Information and Internet Law — Global Practice*, Ch. 5.

6.2.1 Controllers Not in the EU

6.2.1.1 EU Representatives

Under Article 27, if a controller or processor not established in the EU processes personal data of EU residents in relation to the offering of goods or services or monitoring of their behavior (as specified under Article 3(2), then the controller or processor must designate in writing an EU-based representative. The representative must be established in an EU member state where data subjects whose personal data is being processed or behavior monitored are located. The representative must be addressable by DPAs and data subjects on all processing issues related to compliance.

Because the controller or processor is not established within the EU, they cannot take advantage of the lead DPA role (one-stop shop) if they are involved in cross-border data processing activity in the EU. As the WP29 stated, "If the company does not have an establishment in the EU, the mere presence of a representative in a Member State does not trigger the one-stop-shop system. This means that controllers without any establishment in the EU must deal with local supervisory authorities in every Member State they are active in, through their local representative."[14]

6.2.1.2 Representatives vs. DPOs

This then raises the question of whether a non-EU controller or processor could utilize a EU-based DPO to be their representative. The GDPR applies to controllers and processors that process personal data of individuals in the EU, regardless of where the organization is established in the world. Those organizations who are not established inside the EU are required to appoint a representative who is established in the EU for purposes of GDPR compliance. The GDPR also requires a DPO under some circumstances and makes the role voluntary otherwise and the WP29 recommends the DPO be located within the EU for accessibility even if the controller or processor is not. What is this EU representative role, and how does it interplay with the sometimes-overlapping role of the DPO?

Under Article 27, it states that a controller or processor who is not established in the EU and offers goods or services to data subjects in

---

14 Art. 29 DP WP, Guidelines for identifying a controller or processor's lead supervisory authority, r1 (Apr. 2017).

the EU or monitors the behavior of data subjects occurring within the EU must appoint in writing a representative within the EU. On first impression, this representative seems merely to be providing a local point of presence within the EU reached more easily than the non-EU controller or processor. The EU representative is required to be co-located in one of the EU member states with the data subjects who are being offered these goods and services or whose behavior is monitored.

The representative must be available to both the local DPA and data subjects, which makes sense; giving these individuals and supervisory authorities would desire someone nearby who speaks their language and understands their customs and expectations. This seems like the representative role should be one of limited agency, where the EU representative merely takes messages and passes information onto the controller and processor located overseas and then communicates back to the data subject or DPA after receiving instructions from the controller or processor.

Subsection 4 of Article 27 states that the representative "is to be addressed in addition to or instead of the controller or the processor … on all issues related to processing, for the purposes of ensuring compliance with this Regulation." This wording seems to imply that the EU representative may be the only one contacted for GDPR compliance issues if the controller or processor cannot be reached. However, as the DPAs may levy administrative fines and penalties of a significant nature and data subjects may initiate litigation against controllers and processors for damages, the EU representative could find themselves a named party in administrative actions or litigation, as the only defendant that an EU court may be able to obtain effective jurisdiction over.

At least the DPO is protected against legal actions by the data subject and presumably the DPA but similar statutory protection does not appear in the GDPR for the EU representative. Perhaps the presumption was that the EU representative would be an employee of the controller and processor or, at a minimum, an external agent who has contractually limited their liability and specified indemnity by the controller or processor for any issues related to the GDPR. A difficulty for any external agent taking on this role is as the controller or processor is not established within the EU, the agent would have to resort to courts outside the EU if it became necessary to enforce the liability and indemnity clauses of their contract.

Reviewing an earlier draft of the GDPR passed by the European Parliament in 2014 provides some insight. Under the penalties article, it stated that, "Where the controller has established a representative, any penalties shall be applied to the representative, without prejudice to any penalties which could be initiated against the controller." In the final draft of the GDPR, the revised wording has been moved to Recital 80: "The designated representative should be subject to enforcement proceedings in the event of non-compliance by the controller or processor." So, the EU representative may be legally pursued locally for the GDPR noncompliance of overseas entities. Given the limits to the extraterritoriality of laws and the jurisdictional reach of courts, it seems likely the EU representative would be required to at least initially incur the legal and other costs for addressing enforcement actions and be responsible for paying administrative fines and damage suit awards.

What about the line separating the roles of the EU representative and DPO? The earlier draft of the GDPR had required that non-EU controllers and processors appoint a representative in the following situations: where there was "processing of personal data relating to more than 5000 data subjects during any consecutive 12-month period" or there was "processing of special categories of personal data…, location data or data on children or employees in large scale filing systems." This was much of the same criteria that were used to specify when a DPO was required. The final text has revised this to requiring an EU representative for non-EU controllers or processors when offering of goods and services or monitoring the behavior of data subjects, somewhat overlapping the DPO requirement if large-scale regular and systematic monitoring is performed.

The contact details of the EU representative are required to be disclosed to the DPA and to data subjects, just as are the DPO's. The controller's or processor's EU representative is required to maintain a record of processing, which is not a primarily responsibility of a DPO but could be an added task. The EU representative is required to cooperate with the DPA, as are DPOs. In Recital 80, it specifies that the representative is required to "perform its tasks according to the mandate received from the controller or processor," somewhat different than the independence specified for DPOs in performance of their tasks.

So, the DPO and EU representative roles have diverged as the GDPR was revised, but the final text is not completely clear. For example, can a DPO also fulfill the role of EU representative for non-EU controllers and processors? Would any EU-based DPO want to take on this representative role for a non-EU controller or processor, given the potential legal exposures described above? With the uncertain state of the GDPR's final wording, the following query was sent to the Irish DPC: "Can the Article 27 representative of controllers/processors not established in the EU also be the Articles 37–39 Data Protection Officer and if so, how would the representative be shielded from liability from data subjects and the DPC in the same manner that the DPO is?"

The DPC's reply focused on the potential conflicts of interest between the roles, such as in the confidentiality required of the DPO when receiving concerns from employee data subject versus instructions given by the data controller to his representative. Another potential conflict noted was when the DPA is involved in enforcement activities, it would be looking to the DPO to be independent while "the controller and representative are of coequal standing." Another possible conflict could be when the independent DPO role carries out tasks contrary to the instructions given by the controller to the representative role. While the representative may be subject to enforcement proceedings, the DPC did not believe that the representative would be subject to ultimate legal liability under the GDPR, although they should contractually insulate themselves. Due to these potential conflicts, the DPC, while noting that there is no express prohibition on the same person fulfilling both roles, advises caution and notes the controller's responsibility to ensure that the DPO does not take on other tasks that result in a conflict.

6.2.1.3 GDPR DPOs Located Outside the EU

The WP29 has stated[15] that under the GDPR, the accessibility of the DPO must be effective. It regards that accessibility as being effective if the DPO is located within the EU. This is true even if the controller or processor is not located in the EU. It does concede that when the controller or processor has no establishment in the EU, it may be feasible for the DPO to be co-located with the controller or processor outside the EU.

As the DPO has four equal stakeholders they are responsible to, being located outside the EU at the main establishment of the controller or processor may make them more accessible to the board of directors and

---

15 Art. 29 DP WP, Guidelines on Data Protection Officers ("DPOs"), r1 (Apr. 2017).

to the operational personnel in the controller or processor organizations. At the same time, the DPO would be less accessible to the local DPA and to data subjects located within the EU. While anyone can communicate globally via remote messaging and videoconference, it is not the same as speaking the language and understanding the cultural expectations of data subjects and working styles of DPAs. The world is not uni-cultural or uni-lingual, and the remote DPO may find these barriers are significant in accomplishing their responsibilities to remote data subjects and DPAs.

If it is necessary for a DPO to be located outside the EU co-located with the main global establishment of the controller or processor, this would seem to be an ideal example of when the DPO role should be split into at least two individuals: one outside the EU responsible for controller and processor compliance and board communications, and the other inside the EU responsible for data subject communication and DPA coordination.

6.2.2 Other Countries' Privacy Laws

DPOs of multinational organizations based inside the EEA of any organization with global data flows or whose controller or processor is not located inside the EEA will discover that they need to understand privacy laws beyond the GDPR. The following is the briefest of introductions to the privacy laws of countries part of the 20 largest economies in the world outside the EEA. The 20 largest national economies in the world[16] as of 2016 are the United States, China, Japan, Germany, the U.K., France, India, Italy, Brazil, Canada, South Korea, Russia, Australia, Spain, Mexico, Indonesia, Turkey, the Netherlands, Switzerland, and Saudi Arabia. Removing the EU member states leaves 14 countries for discussion.

This list does not represent countries with the best privacy laws, in fact, some of the countries have de minimis privacy protections. Many countries with smaller economies may have more advanced privacy regimes. For larger countries with more rigorous privacy laws, the following discussion still excludes the details of the vast collection of privacy and related laws at the state and territorial levels and the impact of caselaw, which is very important in common law countries. To be able

---

16 The World Bank, GDP (current U.S.$).

to perform any type of compliance activity, the DPO will need a far fuller understanding, including the extraterritoriality of these laws to protect their own citizens. DPOs can start by reading about privacy and security laws from around the world in the companion book.[17] From there, consultation with corporate or independent counsel would be advisable due to the complexity of dealing with multiple legal systems.

6.2.2.1 Americas

The U.S. does not have a general data protection law but instead has a sectoral system of privacy and InfoSec laws that grew up in response to challenges in various industries. Many of these laws date back to the earliest days of the internet era. The most important federal laws for a DPO to become familiar with are HIPAA (health data), GLBA (consumer financial data), FCRA/FACTA (consumer credit data), COPPA (children's data), the FTC Act (authorizes the FTC to act as a privacy regulator), and the Privacy Act (government agency held data and redress by EU citizens). HIPAA and GLBA each have special rules dealing with privacy, security, and data breach. There are other federal laws, including those dealing with education data, communications data, driver's licenses, video rentals, Social Security numbers, and junk email. State laws provide a significant number of privacy and InfoSec protections, such as data breach notification and recovery, online privacy and security, identity theft, phishing, spyware, information security, encryption, secure data disposal, social media credentials, and digital identity. And very significant in a common law country, like the U.S., is the caselaw including class-actions that form another significant source of privacy law protections. Data transfers outside the country are generally not restricted.

Brazil does not have a general data protection law but instead has a constitutional right of privacy based upon the habeas corpus principle. This means that a citizen has the right to have any disputed data noted (not necessarily rectified). There are specific sector laws dealing with the privacy of consumer data, financial information, and children's information. Brazil has no national data protection regulator. Data transfers outside the country are generally not restricted.

Canada has a general data protection called the PIPEDA statute. DPOs must understand that this act only applies to commercial

---

17 Thomas J. Shaw, *Information and Internet Law — Global Practice*, Ch. 2–5.

enterprises, not the national government or nonprofit organizations. That is why the adequacy decision by the EC covered Canada only for commercial aspects of data protection. The Privacy Act addresses government-held data. The provinces and territories have their own most similar privacy laws, including those addressing health data, which apply for data collected within the province. While there are provincial data breach notification requirements, the federal law on breach notification is not yet in force. Canada also has CASL, which addresses junk email and the regulator is the Office of the Privacy Commissioner. Data transfers outside the country are generally not restricted.

Mexico has a general data protection act, Ley Federal de Protección de Datos Personales en Posesión de los Particulares. Based upon European data protection law, it has many of the same features. It also includes a requirement for data breach notification. Transfers to any third party, including those outside the country, require consent. The regulator is the Instituto Nacional de Transparencia, Acceso a la Información y Protección de Datos Personales.

6.2.2.2 Asia/Pacific

China, like the U.S., has no general data protection statute, but instead privacy laws and rules have been added by different governing bodies over time. These include consumer protection, criminal, and tort rules. Privacy rules targeting ISPs and online user data have been implemented. Because of the source of these disparate rules, there is no single national authority for privacy. There is no general data breach notification law. There are laws requiring the processing of data collected within China to remain within China.

Japan has a general data protection statute, the Personal Information Protection Act. Revisions have placed restrictions on overseas transfers unless the receiving country has adequate data protection and applies the act to that transferred data. Personal data cannot be transferred to a third party without consent without specific derogations. There is no express data breach notification, but there are numerous industry guidelines. Regulatory oversight is split between the Personal Information Protection Commission and industry-specific regulators. Japan is in discussion with the EC over the adequacy of its data protection regime.

India does not have a general data protection statute but instead relies upon regulations under the IT Act, and the right to privacy was recently found in its constitution. This act is directed at cybercrime, but the Information Technology (Reasonable Security Practices and Procedures and Sensitive Personal Data or Information) Rules include general privacy principles and applies to private sector organizations processing data inside India. Overseas data flows are not restricted unless the data is sensitive. India does not have a national privacy regulator.

The Republic of (South) Korea has a general data protection statute, the revised Act of Promotion of Information and Communication Network Utilization and Information Protection. Data breach notification is required. Consent is required for cross-border data transfers. The privacy regulator is the Personal Information Protection Commission. South Korea is in discussion with the EC over the adequacy of its data protection regime.

Australia has a general data protection statute, the revised Privacy Act, which follows the Australian Privacy Principles. Any entity transferring the personal data of Australians out of the country must ensure that the recipient complies with these privacy principles. The states and territories in Australia also have passed privacy laws. Data breach notification is now required. The Spam Act deals with junk email. The Office of the Australian Information Commissioner is the national regulator.

Indonesia does not have a general data protection statute. Privacy law is based on two e-commerce statutes and the constitution. Those laws are enforced by the Ministry of Communication and Information. There are no clear restrictions on overseas data transfers.

Asia-Pacific also has a regional privacy forum through the Asia Pacific Economic Cooperation, a group of 21 countries and territories in Asia and the Americas that borders the Pacific Ocean. This has three important aspects, starting with the APEC Privacy Framework, which is a voluntary privacy scheme that serves as a kind of model law for countries' privacy statutes with a defined set of privacy principles. The Cross-Border Privacy Rules allow for the transfer of personal information among these countries according to the privacy principles in the framework and other local privacy laws. Accountability agents certify organizations as personal information controllers against those rules. The Privacy Recognition for Processors is a trustmark designation for personal information processors whose policies and practices are evaluated by an accountability agent as helping a controller comply with the framework and the rules.

6.2.2.3 Other

Russia does not have a general data protection statute but instead has the law On Personal Data. A data localization law requires that data collected about Russian nationals in Russia remain in the country. The Communications, IT and Mass Media ministry is responsible for these laws. Data transfers overseas are allowed only to countries with adequate privacy regimes. As a member of the Council of Europe, Russia has ratified ETS no. 108 (Convention for the Protection of Individuals with regard to Automatic Processing of Personal Data).

Turkey has a new general data protection statute, the Data Protection Law. This law was based upon the EU's DPD, which would limit the overseas transfer of data. The national regulator is the Persona Data Protection Board. As a member of the Council of Europe, Turkey has ratified ETS no. 108 (Convention for the Protection of Individuals with regard to Automatic Processing of Personal Data).

Switzerland does have a general data protection statute, the Federal Data Protection Act. Overseas transfers of personal data require adequacy of the receiving data protection regime. The U.S. and Switzerland entered into a Privacy Shield agreement similar to that between the EU and U.S. Switzerland's data protection regime has been the subject of an adequacy decision from the EC. The government is planning to revise the data privacy law to be more attuned to the GDPR.

Saudi Arabia does not have a general data protection statute. This means that data protection would be interpreted under Shariah principles, which has a right of privacy. If not specifically stated, courts may determine what is appropriate. There are certain privacy protections under the health and telecommunications laws.

6.2.2.4 DPOs Under Other Countries' Privacy Laws

DPOs are not unique to EU data protection law. Other countries may require DPO roles, although the legal responsibilities vary. For example, in Canada, a person must be designated who is responsible for compliance with PIPEDA. In Mexico, a person must be designated to deal with data subject requests and promote the protection of data within the organization. In Singapore, under the Personal Data Protection Act, DPOs are required to be designated to be responsible for compliance with the law, oversee data protection activities in the organization, handle DP complaints and inquiries, and cooperate with the local DPA.

As previously mentioned, DPOs under the GDPR should not be legally subject to data subjects or administrative fines from DPAs but may be liable for professional negligence or ethical violations. The IAPP analyzed the role of DPOs in several countries[18] and found that they may be subject to civil or criminal liability when acting in their roles. The report listed Canada, Hong Kong, Ireland, Malaysia, the Philippines, Singapore, and the U.K. as jurisdictions where corporate officers or those involved in various aspects of data protection can be held civil and criminally liable and even imprisoned for DP-related offenses. It recommends E&O and data breach insurance coverage in any event to address liability arising from civil suits. Criminal liability would likely not be covered by this insurance.

---

18 IAPP, Legal risks to being a DPO (Sept. 2017).

CHAPTER 7

Putting It All Together — Example Scenarios

The prior six chapters have detailed the individual components describing how a DPO is qualified and engaged; the role defined, the initial tasks performed; GDPR compliance audited; risk, DPIAs, and technical assessments on InfoSec; data breach response; and privacy by design and data transfers outside the EEA are handled. To bring all these together, this chapter closes the book be using the example of two mythical organizations that process the personal data of EU residents and how the organizations' DPO goes about their role from Day 1. This should tie together these many tasks and hopefully point out many of the pitfalls that DPOs can encounter in their practices.

The two organizations are a large international company and a small- and medium-sized enterprise. Both organizations will evaluate whether they need a DPO and how to source one (Chapters 1 and 2), how the DPO evaluates GDPR compliance (Chapter 3), how the DPO performs the technical assessments (Chapters 4 and 5), and how they evaluate data transfer safeguards (Chapter 6). These scenarios are highly simplified and telegraph the DP issues from a long way off but show the DPOs in action addressing issues they would have to address in the real world. Each presents different aspects and tasks of the DPO role, although a real DPO must deal with all tasks every time.

DPO Areas of Focus

- Initiate the DPO role — SME and multinational
- Assess GDPR compliance — SME and multinational
- Perform technical assessments — SME and multinational
- Assess transfers outside the EEA — SME and multinational

7.1 Leaping Unicorns Ltd. — SME

7.1.1 Leaping Unicorn's Situation

7.1.1.1 Business Details

The firm of Leaping Unicorns Ltd. (LUL) is an EU small- and middle-sized enterprise (SME). Its headquarters are in Ireland, and it has locations in Lichtenstein and France. The firm is in the business of exporting consumer electronics products made by its French subsidiary to other countries inside and outside the EU. Sales and marketing of the products are handled out of the Lichtenstein office, which sells to other companies as a wholesaler and sells directly to consumers by its website. It averages 50,000 online customers globally with 15,000 buying something every year. The firm is planning to soon introduce a new technology that allows for the delivery of its products by drones. They also intend to use a facial recognition technology to validate to whom to deliver a package, but this new technology is still in the design phase.

7.1.1.2 Personal Data Details

When selling to consumers on its website, LUL asks the buyer to supply their name, address, bank card details, age, and favorite singer, in addition to a digital photo. The data is stored on a cloud data server hosted by U.S. firm EasyStore and mirrored to its servers in Canada. LUL adds the data to its customer database, from which marketing promotions are sometimes generated, based on prior purchases or products searched on its website. The address is used to ship the goods ordered, and the bank card details are used to process payment for the goods. A digital template is created from the photo to use for the planned facial recognition feature.

7.1.2 Introducing/Initiating the DPO Role

7.1.2.1 Is a DPO Mandatory or Voluntary?

LUL must first determine if a DPO is mandatory or voluntary. As it is not a public authority, a DPO would be mandatory, according to Chapter 1, only if there was regular and systematic monitoring on a large scale or processing of special categories of data on a large scale. There are at least two uses of personal data that may fall within these criteria. The first is that LUL is using data gathered from its customers' use of its website to generate marketing outreach. To do so, they must have been systematically monitoring the behavior of these users while they were on their website. The second is the use of the digital template created from the photos, which may be considered biometric data under the GDPR and therefore a special category of data that is intended to be used on a large scale for package delivery.

When analyzing these two requirements, LUL believes that both the collecting and processing of website activity information and the use of digital templates to verify its delivery recipients would likely fall within its core activities, as both are part of the systems used to market and deliver their revenue-producing services. But LUL is not sure if their processing is sufficiently large scale to requirement them to hire a mandatory DPO, so it looks at the factors from Chapter 1: the number of data subjects involved, the volume of data, the different types of data, the permanence of the processing, and the geographic scope of the processing. With 50,000 data subjects globally and 15,000 new online sales a year, this seems like it could be large-scale processing, but it is still not definitively clear. LUL determines that it would be best to designate a DPO voluntarily, even if is not mandatory, to promote customer confidence in its new technologies and so documents this analysis, knowing that a voluntary DPO has all the same legal obligations as a mandatory DPO.

7.1.2.2 Insourcing versus Outsourcing

LUL then reviews the job skills for a DPO listed in Chapter 1 but quickly determines that it does not have any available person on its staff with the required skill set. LUL then must determine if it should hire an external candidate or outsource the role. The benefits of hiring their own person is that they could learn the business processes of LUL and get to know its data processing in great detail. The downside is that there is a cost to pay an agency to locate an external resource, assuming they could identify a suitably qualified candidate. But more than that, LUL is not sure how much of a DPO they require, as they are an SME with limited resources.

Using the criteria listed in Chapter 2, they evaluate, qualify, and select David, a well-reputed and experienced privacy lawyer, to handle their DPO function on a part-time basis, with the ability to add hours if needed. Outsourcing the role also assures LUL that David is less likely to have conflicts of interest and be able to perform his role in an independent manner. They also get access to a talented professional that would have been very expensive to hire full time and can let his DPO hours grow if needed with the sales growth of LUL. David explained that, in his experience, much of the important work of a DPO comes in the initial compliance assessment and then follow-ups on the remediation plan. So part time is an appropriate DPO arrangement for LUL.

The firm notifies the Irish DPA, as well as those in France and Lichtenstein, of David's designation as DPO and announces it internally to all staff members. His contact details are added to the external data protection statement and internally to the data protection policy. David is to report into the board of directors and provide an annual report of his activities and findings. Being a lawyer, they do not provide him with additional budget for outside counsel but do make one of their internal auditors a part-time member of his DPO team. He is given access rights to all necessary documents and systems and is added to the schedules of relevant meetings and reviews.

7.1.3 Assessing GDPR Compliance

7.1.3.1 Compliance with DP Principles

David begins his role by interviewing top management, looking for their commitment to both data protection for the firm as a whole and to his role in assessing their compliance with the GDPR. He reviews the available documentation and follows up with data and process owners and specialists when he cannot find the answers, leaving them the tasks to update the documentation with the newly discovered information. He will use the data protection policy and the data and processing inventory and related supporting policies and procedures. At this time, he is not overly concerned about doing a formal audit or insisting upon evidence to support each policy or procedure as a formal audit would. Instead the initial assumption is that the policy or procedure or technology works as designed.

Using the initial assessment checklist and questions from Chapter 3, he will first evaluate how LUL meets its obligations for the seven DP principles. Turning first to the data and processing inventory, it should state (or will after it is revised) that the personal data collected directly from customers is name, address, address, bank card details, age, favorite singer, and a digital photo. Personal data not collected directly includes their website browsing activity, perhaps their IP address or device identifier, and the digital template of their photo.

The processing activities should show that all the directly collected data was collected and stored. The other personal data was taken from examining their browsing activity perhaps by using a cookie, IP address, device identifier, or all of them. The digital template was created by the process of digitizing the analog photo provided by the customer. The sales process uses at least the name and bank card details, and the delivery process uses the name, address, and soon the digital template. Marketing uses the online history for digital and other advertising. Other process activities, such as system backups, are assumed to take place regularly.

Against these lists, the seven DP principles can be applied to against each of the processing operations to understand how compliant the controller is. These DP principles should also be stated in the publicly available DP statement. Just considering the first processing operation, collection, would generate these inquiries:

P1: Was the processing lawful, fair, and transparent? To check this, David must ascertain first the legal basis for the collection processing. It would be expected that it was based either upon consent or the processing of a contract, but LUL should have documented which. If consent, what procedures did LUL have to know that the consent was unambiguous, specific, informed, and freely given? Was there an online process that demonstrated the customer unambiguously agreeing to the collection of their personal data? Was the consent explicit for the biometric data (was it biometric data yet, see article in the Appendix)? Was a record kept of the consent received? How did LUL inform its customers sufficiently to gain consent? How does LUL know that the consent was freely given? If the collection processing is based upon performance of a contract, is all the personal data collected necessary for the performance of the contract (e.g., age)? For fairness and transparency, were data subjects provided all the information required in Articles 13 and 14 for the data that was collected directly and indirectly from them?

P2: Was the collection for a specified, explicit, and legitimate purpose? Did LUL document an internal assessment that it did for the specified purpose of the collection? Did LUL perform a compatibility assessment for any further processing it contemplated after the collection (remember that further processing and a processing for a different purpose are not the same thing)? Is it clear and unambiguous what the purpose of the processing is? Is the processing compliant with all relevant laws? What are all the laws that the collection processing must be compliant with? Was marketing to customers and website users a stated purpose of collection?

P3: Is data minimized through processing only what is adequate, relevant, and necessary for the purposes? For the purposes for which it was collected, is each type of personal data relevant and necessary (e.g., age, favorite singer)? If it is not necessary for ordering, payment, and delivery of electronic goods, why was it collected? Is there another purpose, and was that purpose disclosed to the customer? If the data is found to be not necessary, is it immediately deleted?

P4: Is personal data accurate and up to date? What procedures does LUL have to keep data accurate (input controls and software application integrity controls to check data types)? What controls does LUL have to keep data up to date (re-verifying information provided by the customer, process by which they can update the information stored about them)? How do data subject requests for rectification get handled?

P5: Is personal data kept no longer than necessary? Is there a data retention policy and period for each type of personal data collected? What triggers the erasure of data from a system? What procedures are there for sweeping the system to determine if any data is retained beyond its retention periods?

P6: Is security appropriate to prevent unauthorized loss or disclosure of personal data? Are there InfoSec assessments performed as in Chapter 5? (This will be analyzed in detail in the second scenario.)

P7: Can the controller demonstrate compliance with P1–P6? Is there documented evidence, for every type of personal data processed and every type of processing activity undertaken, that LUL has complied with the GDPR principles?

7.1.3.2 Compliance with Other Obligations

Beyond complying with DP principles, LUL must have processes to respond to the exercising of data subject rights. These rights should be stated in the public DP statement, including the availability of these rights, how they are exercised by data subjects, and how they are responded to by the firm. David must check how requests are communicated and handled for access to a data subject's personal data under Article 15; rectifying or erasing their personal data under Articles 16 and 17; restricting, objecting to, or not being subject to certain automated processing of their personal data under Articles 18, 21, and 22; and porting of their personal data under Article 20, as well as how complaints are handled. There must be appropriate procedures for identifying a data subject before honoring these requests.

Controllers must have kept a record of the data processing activities. David must check when these records are created and updated regarding processing activities and what information is being recorded per the Article 30 requirements. David must also ascertain what other data protection requirements beyond the GDPR that LUL is required to comply with and discover when and how that compliance. At a minimum, the storage of cookies on their customers' computers would imply ePrivacy Directive obligations. Use of the customers' details to reach out to them with direct marketing communications would fall under the ePrivacy Directive, so who these are sent to (new or existing customers) and format of the messages should be verified. LUL would also be subject to at least employment and consumer protection laws in Ireland, France, and Lichtenstein that may have data protection implications, plus possibly data protection laws with extraterritorial application for protection of its non-EU citizens.

7.1.4 Technical Assessments

7.1.4.1 DPIAs

LUL is planning to introduce drones to provide delivery services for its products ordered by customers. These drones would use video cameras to be directed by an operator to the address of their scheduled delivery. Use of video recording in public areas can have significant data protection implications. Because this is a new technology involving personal data processed in a new and potentially invasive manner, David advises that, per Article 35, a data protection impact assessment should be undertaken before this new service commences. Evaluating the different types of methodologies, David advises using the DPIA methodology from CNIL, as he believes that it is the most comprehensive, as discussed in Chapter 4.

As LUL performs the DPIA, David monitors its progress and findings. He advises LUL that it must focus on minimizing the impact of the invasive use of the video taken by the drone by having the drone travel upon public roads so that the camera is viewing only the road and related street signs and is at no time looking into private residences, schools, hospitals, and similar institutions. David advises that the video is not recorded by LUL, despite LUL believing that it would need to keep a recording for legal lability purposes. The operator of the drone is advised to be adequately trained in data protection principles and the viewing screen of the operator not be viewable by anyone else. David also advises that acknowledgement of delivery is done outside the delivery process, via email, such that the drone itself is not carrying any personal data. If his recommendations are carried out, David believes these measures will treat the risk sufficiently to not result in a high risk to data subjects, but he believes it is best to reach out and notify the Irish DPC as a matter of good practice, as well as DPAs in all EU countries where such drone deliveries will take place.

7.1.4.2 PbD

LUL is also planning to use a facial recognition capability during deliveries to match the face of the product buyer with the person who receives delivery but is in the design stage of this technology. David must advise LUL on the data protection opportunities to install privacy into this technology at this early phase. David meets with the designers of this technology and explains the seven foundational principles of PbD from IPC and the eight design strategies from ENISA, as discussed in Chapter 5. They decide that they should minimize the data, not retain it, provide notice, and use encryption to further safeguard the personal data and to set this as the default.

To minimize the data, they analyze the program used in this new technology to create a digital template from live image of the data subject and determine that they can use less data points to extract the needed facial features to match the digital template they created from the uploaded photo of the data subject. Second, a decision is made to never store the image of a data subject taken by the new technology when delivery is made and to delete this new digital template after it is confirmed against the existing digital template. Third, all images and digital templates are encrypted within the new technology, and the keys are securely managed. Fourth, data subjects are notified of this use of facial recognition software when the product is being ordered and when the delivery is scheduled, with the ability to not participate in this manner. Fifth, data subjects are offered the ability to have their original photo they uploaded during the order process deleted upon successful creation of the digital template. Six, pseudonymization of the link between the digital template and the name of the customer will be employed as much as possible.

David determines he is satisfied that these PbD actions will decrease the risks to data subjects for disclosure of their personal data, including sensitive data, in the implementation of this new technology. As the technology gets closer to implementation, he will perform a DPIA and again, as good practice, he will seek to verify his assessment with the relevant DPAs.

7.1.5 Data Transfers

7.1.5.1 Processor Agreement

The personal data is transferred outside the EEA to be stored on servers in the U.S. and Canada. David must ascertain the safeguards that are in place for these transfers. The first is the controller-processor agreement between LUL and cloud storage EasyStore. Does the agreement conform to the requirements of the GDPR, or is it just a standard set of T&Cs

provided to cloud storage as a service customer? Under Article 28, David must ascertain that the agreement has sufficient guarantees to protect the rights of its EU data subjects. The processor here is merely storing the data and undertakes no other processing besides mirroring the data to its Canada server, so the agreement should be clear that those are its only processing activities and will undertake none without express instructions from LUL.

The agreement should clearly articulate its commitment to data protection/privacy principles for EU personal data, including a publicly available privacy policy. Its employees and contractors should be bound by confidentiality agreements. It should note its commitment to InfoSec, have a link to its InfoSec and DP policies, and explain the InfoSec standards certifications it has achieved. What happens to data stored with it upon termination of services should be clearly spelled out in the agreement, including secure deletion of data, in both countries where the data is stored. Notifications upon events, such as security incidents, data breach, bankruptcy, and sale of the company, should be described. Liability for any impacts on data subjects and any limits should also be expressly stated, as well as the right to audit or use of its audited reports.

David must not only review the controller-processor agreement for the details as described in Chapter 3, but also read through any referenced DP and InfoSec policies/statements, as described in Chapters 2 and 5 respectively, looking for potential issues. With the agreement assessed, David can then review the data transfer mechanism.

7.1.5.2 Adequacy/Privacy Shield

As Ireland, France, and Lichtenstein are all within the EEA, there is no need to deal with a transfer mechanism between those countries. However, transferring data to the U.S. and then onward to Canada requires David to understand the requirements of the Privacy Shield for the U.S. transfers and the adequacy decision for the Canada transfers. For EasyStore to be self-certified under the Privacy Shield, it must have committed to the privacy principles as described in Chapter 6, which are legal obligations upon their joining that program. This also provides for accountability for onward transfer and recourse mechanism for EU residents, including use of their local DPAs. LUL's membership can easily be verified by checking the U.S. Department of Commerce's list of companies under the Privacy Shield.

David should also review EasyStore's privacy policy required as part of the Privacy Shield program. David would look at the EC's adequacy decision for Canada and see that it only applies to commercial transfers of data, which should cover LUL's commercial transfer of this data. As adequacy decision do not require specific authorization from DPAs, allowing for the ongoing transfers of this personal data outside the EEA. While the EC has determined that these countries data protection regimes are adequate as described, this personal data is now being processed under different privacy laws. As such, David show review the relevant privacy laws in the U.S. and Canada as introduced in Chapter 6 to determine any potential impacts on the rights and freedoms of the EU data subjects.

With these activities, David has now performed an initial high-level assessment of LUL's compliance with the GDPR, including DPIAs and PbD for new technologies, and can make a report that establishes a baseline level of compliance. He should have discussed and set in motion remediations in every area where he found a compliance gap and set the stage for his future audits where evidence will need to be produced to demonstrate compliance with GDPR and all relevant statutes and policies. David must stay involved in all DP issues inside the organization and watch for changes to relevant legislation, standards, and technologies.

7.2 Exhilarating Elephants Inc. — Multinational

7.2.1 Exhilarating Elephants' Situation

7.2.1.1 Business Details

The company of Exhilarating Elephants Inc. (EEI) is a U.S. multinational with EU subsidiaries and 50 million subscribers and an Indian processor for application development (Hyperbad) and a Philippine processor for mirroring and disaster recovery (QuikBakk). Its headquarters are in California, and it has global locations, including in Germany and Italy. The company is in the social media business, hosting its websites in Germany and California. The Italian location provides the design of future website software apps and marketing for the EU. The company offers consumers who use its websites special discounts for referring friends who become subscribers. It also gives a monthly free subscription to the user who clicks the "meh" button the most times for each of its new "crazy drama" videos put out by fellow subscribers. It also provides to other websites a social app plug-in with a "trumpet" icon in the shape of an elephant's trunk to show that a user intends to remember the "trumpeted" webpage forever.

7.2.1.2 Personal Data Details

Personal data is collected from subscribers to EEI when the user registers, providing their name, address, phone number, email user id, number of siblings, gender, age, race, and education level. Children under the age of 13 are not allowed to register unless Mom or Dad says it is fine by clicking the "A-OK" button. Personal data is also collected by the activity of subscribers on the website, such as when they post a "crazy drama" video or on another site when they click the "trumpet" button. Personal data of non-subscribers, such as referred friends and those hitting the "trumpet" button, is also gathered. Unhappy with all this data collection, several of its customers have asked for their data subject rights under Articles 15–22. A data breach has recently occurred requiring notice under Article 34 for which EEI provided notifications to subscribers but not to any other data subjects.

7.2.2 Introducing/Initiating the DPO Role

7.2.2.1 Is a DPO Required/Outsourcing?

EEI must first determine if a DPO is mandatory or voluntary. As it is not a public authority, a DPO would be mandatory, according to Chapter 1, only if there was regular and systematic monitoring on a large scale or processing of special categories of data on a large scale. EEI seems to meet both criteria. First, it monitors the use of its social media site by its 50 million subscribers in several ways. It also monitors the "trumpets" of non-subscribers. Second, it collects information from subscribers when registering that falls into the special categories of personal data under Article 9 (e.g., race). As these are core activities of its business and by any measure large scale, it is clear that EEI is mandated to designate a DPO, it concurs with that conclusion, and so documents this DPO requirement analysis.

7.2.2.2 Insourcing versus Outsourcing

EEI then reviews the job skills for a DPO listed in Chapter 1 and realizes that it has the perfect internal candidate. Upon being approached, she quickly makes it clear that she will be on maternity leave for at least the next year. EEI determines that it does not have any other available person on its EU staff with the required skill set, but it does have a promising candidate, Helen, who would need a few years under an experienced DPO. She resides in the U.S. but would relocate to the EU to take on this role. EEI calculates that costs of using a part-time DPO mentor plus their internal younger DPO trainee would be about the same as using the existing but unavailable internal candidate. So, they look to outsource the DPO mentor role.

Using the criteria listed in Chapter 2, they evaluate, qualify, and select Dieter, a well-reputed and experienced compliance auditor, to act part time as a mentor and prepare Helen to take over this DPO function within two years. By outsourcing the role, Dieter is less likely to have conflicts of interest, and Helen is given no other duties that could raise a conflict of interest. He will be the designated DPO the first year and then, if ready, Helen will be designated in the second year with Dieter mentoring her. The company notifies the German and Italian DPAs of Dieter's designation and announces it internally to all staff members in the EU and the U.S. His contact details are added to the external data protection statement and internally to the data protection policy. Dieter is to report into the board of directors and provide a quarterly report of his activities and findings. Helen is to report to Dieter only. Not being a lawyer, EEI provides Dieter with a budget for outside EU legal counsel, but Helen's legal experience in the U.S. will greatly assist the DPO team in dealing with global privacy laws.

7.2.3 Assessing GDPR Compliance

7.2.3.1 Compliance with DP Principles

Dieter initiates his role, in tandem with Helen, by interviewing top management, data and process owners, and reviewing available documentation, including the data and processing inventory and the data protection policy, as in Chapter 2. Dieter is of the opinion, given the vast number and global dispersion of its subscribers, that the data protection policy publicly available on EEI's website is of vital importance in not only laying out the DP obligations of EEI and the DP rights of its subscribers, but also in communicating how the personal data of all affected individuals is processed and eventually deleted.

The DP policy has the following sections: Purpose, FIPPs, Security, Cookies, Data Collected and Used, and Changes to the Policy. The FIPPs section articulates the FTC's Fair Information Practice Principles. The Security section states that EEI uses state of the art security to protect subscribers' data. Dieter recommends that the DP policy be revised to be a global best practice, using the GDPR's obligations and rights as the basis for all EEI's data protection practices globally. His proposed revision of the DP policy would include a Scope section; DP principles and DS rights sections; DPO contact details; sections on disclosure, retention, and deletion of personal data; sections on how processing of sensitive data and children's data is handled; and the InfoSec section would be expanded to further elaborate on safeguards implemented across the company and standards certification earned.

Using the checklist and questions from Chapter 3, Dieter then evaluates how EEI meets its obligations for the seven DP principles. The data and processing inventory should show the personal data collected directly from subscribers is name, address, phone number, email user id, number of siblings, gender, age, race, and education level. Personal data not collected directly includes their social media website activity, such as posting "crazy drama" video, "meh-ing" a video, "trumpeting" another webpage, and perhaps their IP address or device identifier. Personal data is also collected from non-subscribers, such as the name and contact details of referred friends or the IP address or device identifier for those using the "trumpet" or "meh" buttons, and children's parent's name and contact details when using the "A-OK" button.

The processing activities should show that all the directly collected data was collected and stored during the registration process. The other personal data was taken from examining their website activity in "meh-ing" a "crazy drama" video or clicking the "trumpet," "meh," or "A-OK" buttons perhaps by using a cookie, IP address, device identifier, or all of them. Referred friends contact details would be processed when they are invited to join. Parents' contact details and those of their under-age-13 child would be processed when a verification email is sent to the parent.

Other processing activities, such as system backups, are assumed to take place regularly.

Against the data and processing lists, supporting documentation and interviews with owners and specialists, the seven DP principles can be applied to against each of the processing operations to understand how compliant the EEI is. Just considering the first processing operation, collection, would generate these inquiries:

P1: Was the processing lawful, fair, and transparent? Dieter must ascertain the legal basis for the collection processing, and there are quite a few different places where data is collected. When the data was collected online during subscriber registration, how was the consent unambiguous, specific, informed, and freely given? Did the subscriber click on an "I accept" button after being informed of the purposes of the processing? How was the user clicking on the "meh," "trumpet," and "OK" buttons made aware of the fact their personal data is being processed? How did they consent? Were records kept of this consent? Were there any coercive or hidden aspects to the registration process to negate it being freely given? If EEI believes that the collection processing is based upon performance of a contract for subscribers, is all the personal data collected necessary for the performance of the contract (e.g., number of siblings, gender, age, race, and education level)? What about non-subscribers?

Under Article 8, collection of personal data of children under the age of 16, unless modified by member state statute, requires parental consent reasonably verified by the controller. How does EEI enforce the varying ages of digital consent in each EU country? How does it reasonably verify parental consent? For fairness and transparency, were data subjects provided all the information required in Articles 13 and 14 for the data that was collected directly and indirectly from them?

P2: Was the collection for a specified, explicit, and legitimate purpose? Some of the data collected looks like what might be needed to add the users as a subscriber. Other collected data items look like they were added to advertise to the subscriber. Still others were collected from their website activity. Did EEI document the internal assessment that it undertook for the specified purpose(s) of the collection? Did EEI perform a compatibility assessment for any further processing it contemplated after the collection (remember that further processing and a processing for a different purpose are not the same thing)? Is it clear and unambiguous what the purpose(s) of the processing is? Is the processing compliant with all relevant laws? What are all the laws that the collection processing must be compliant with?

P3: Is data minimized through processing only what is adequate, relevant, and necessary for the purposes? For the purposes for which it was collected, is each type of personal data relevant and necessary (e.g., number of siblings, gender, age, race, and education level)? If it is not necessary for being part of the social media site, why was that personal data type collected? Is there another purpose (e.g., advertising), and was that purpose disclosed to the customer? If the data is found to be not necessary, is it immediately deleted?

P4: Is personal data is accurate and up to date? What procedures does EEI have to keep data accurate (input controls, application controls to check data types, database record types)? What controls does EEI have to keep data up to date (re-verifying information provided by the customer, process by which they can update the information stored about them)? How do data subject requests for rectification get handled?

P5: Is personal data kept no longer than necessary? Is there a data retention policy and period for each type of personal data collected? What triggers the erasure of personal data from a system? What procedures are there for sweeping the system to determine if any personal data is retained beyond its retention periods? What legal obligations are there for retaining data for a specified period? What is the impact on potential or actual litigation on the retention or deletion of personal data?

P6: Is security appropriate to prevent unauthorized loss or disclosure of personal data? Are there InfoSec assessments or certifications performed? (This will be analyzed in the technical assessment below.)

P7: Can the controller demonstrate compliance with P1–P6? Is there documented evidence, for every type of personal data processed and every type of processing activity undertaken, that EEI has complied with its obligations under the GDPR for these DP principles (see Chapter 3)?

7.2.3.2 Compliance with Other Obligations

EEI is required to be able to respond within limited time frame to data subject's exercise of their DP rights. The time frames are established under Article 12 as being within one month unless the controller needs more time and then informs the requestor within one month of this. Does EEI have a process set up and fully explained publicly in their DP policy to allow data subjects to initiate requests under their DP rights to access (Article 15), rectification (Article 16), erasure (Article 17), restricting processing (Article 18), porting their personal data (Article 20), objecting to processing (Article 21), and not being subject to decisions made solely upon automated processing (Article 22)? The existing requests made by data subjects would provide evidence of how the response mechanism currently operates, which Dieter should inspect.

How does EEI keep track of these requests and ensure their timely completion? How does EEI verify the identity of the requestor to know what personal data is applicable? How does the EEI keep track of all personal data that applies to each data subject? What type of restrictions are provided for in local law in Germany, Italy, and other EU countries regarding these data subject rights? Are there member state or EU laws restricting what data can be erased and what personal data does this apply to? In what electronic formats is ported personal data made available? Has EEI set up the ability to port data directly to other controllers? Does EEI make any automated decisions that affect the rights of its data subjects? Dieter must look closely at the processes set up for data subject rights and the relevant restrictions on those rights and time frames, along with any past evidence of the exercising of data subject rights.

Dieter must check when the records of processing activities per the Article 30 requirements. Dieter must also ascertain what other data protection provisions that EEI is required to comply with in the EU, the U.S., and elsewhere and how compliance with these laws is verified and any relevant regulatory investigations. Dieter should also check the type of data protection training provided to specialists and the DP awareness efforts within the company and to relevant contractors and vendors. And the mechanisms that the company uses to stay abreast of changes to the law and technology related to data protection in each relevant jurisdiction.

7.2.4 Technical Assessments

7.2.4.1 InfoSec

The InfoSec capabilities of EEI are an extremely important aspect for the protection of data subject rights, given the vast amount of personal data held by the controller. So, Dieter decides that, while there are other approaches, the best InfoSec assessment for EEI would be a combination of the ISO certification process and the ISO and NIST control catalogs, set on top of a risk assessment methodology based on the ISO standard for InfoSec risk. In assessing InfoSec risk, Dieter will assess both the controller EEI and their two processors Hyperbad and QuikBakk. Dieter must review documents from all three companies and interview specialists in the EU, the U.S., India, and the Philippines, remotely or in person.

Dieter first reviews the risk management programs against ISO 27005 (see Chapter 4). This requires that there be an ongoing program to assess and treat InfoSec risk. In the context establishment phase, the organizational, geographic, and business process scope of the risk program must be defined. Along with that, each organization must have established criteria for determining how critical an information asset is, the impact of the loss or disclosure of, and amount of residual risk that can be accepted.

The risk assessment phase must show an established program that accomplishes all the following. It must identify and value the business assets that InfoSec is protecting; it must be able to identify threats, existing controls to deal with those threats, vulnerabilities, and the consequences if a threat exploits a vulnerability. Threat identification is an ongoing process and multifaceted, looking for threats externally and internally, from hackers, criminals, disgruntled employees, competitors, and perhaps, most frequently, negligence from poor training. Technical tools, published lists, knowledge-sharing networks, and outside experts can all be sources of the types of threats an organization might face. Vulnerability identification can occur using scanning tools, published lists, and code, process, or contract walkthroughs.

Dieter needs to discover how an organization identifies the InfoSec threats and vulnerabilities that it faces then how it analyzes the consequences (severity) and likelihood of a threat exploiting a vulnerability and how often it runs risk assessments and their scope. From there, risks must be treated by either avoiding, transferring, retaining, or reducing the risk with controls, which is discussed below. A comprehensive risk register with regular risk assessments based on the above or similar methodology across the whole scope of the enterprise, periodic meetings to discuss the status of risk treatments, and reviews of the effectiveness of implemented controls would be a minimum that Dieter should expect at each organization.

He then reviews each company as if he was performing an ISO 27001 certification (see Chapter 5). Has each of the organizations established an information security management system, and how is it supported by top management through objectives, roles, and commitments (ISMS)? Is there in InfoSec policy, and how is it and a security culture integrated into the organization's processes? Has the risk management program been established organization wide? How aware are employees and contractors are of the ISMS, and how do they contribute to its effectiveness? How does the organization monitor changes to risk and the IS systems? How is the effectiveness of the ISMS evaluated? How often are internal audits and management reviews undertaken? How are nonconformities addressed, and what is the process for continual improvement?

Finally, he considers the actual InfoSec controls selected to treat risks identified in the risk assessment exercises (see Chapter 5). The ISO 27002 catalog of controls provides the general areas that should exist in any ISMS and so the existence of each control in the 14 control categories should be noted and any missing controls justified. The categories were InfoSec policy, organization, HR, asset management, access control, cryptography, physical and environmental, operations, communications, systems development, suppliers, incident management, business continuity, and compliance. The ISO controls should be supplemented by the list of NIST controls for added depth.

For this initial assessment, Dieter does not need to assess the effectiveness of the controls or find evidence — that will occur later during a formal audit, although any obvious issues with control effectiveness should be addressed now. He should note every risk has been appropriately treated, and for those risks that are being reduced, he should note the controls and how they map to the specifically addressing the risks of a global social media website with multiple hosting locations with real-time data transfers and many different entry points into the system for personal data collection and access.

7.2.4.2 Data Breach

The data breach response processes for all three organizations needs to be evaluated by Dieter. He is looking holistically at the incident response process, for which data breach is one type of response and within data breach one of the action items is compliance with statutory breach notifications. The first item is for Dieter to gain an understand of how the organizations have defined a personal data breach, meaning which type of incidents will lead to something that it classifies as a breach that impacts the confidentiality, integrity, an availability of personal data, and so triggers the data breach response process. He may find this by reading the incident response policies and procedures, or it may be detailed separately in data breach process documents. The actual data breach that has occurred should be examined, including how risk to data subjects was evaluated.

The questions detailed in Chapter 5 must then be answered, including the identification of the types and classifications of personal data an organization has, their present storage locations, and whether the data is encrypted? If encryption is used, what is type, and how are the encryption keys managed and safeguarded? What technologies are deployed to notify the organization of a potential data breach? How will a security incident be classified as a data breach, and what processes are used to determine what has happened to the personal data (alternation, loss, access)? What severity levels have been predefined? Who is allocated the responsibility to call a security incident a data breach, and what if they are not available? Who are the members of the incident response team, and what are their respective skill sets? Have the exact steps in the breach response process been clearly defined, and how has the response process been tested?

For the processor organizations and any part of their data that EEI has stored with third-party service providers, such as cloud providers, Dieter would need to make the following additional inquires. For encrypted data, who at the service providers has access to the keys? What is the key management process? Is the data of multiple customers stored upon the same physical devices? How can they determine affected data in event of a breach? What are their intrusion detection and prevention tools and techniques? How do they define a breach? Is EEI notified of all security incidents? How is access provided to the data and facilities in the event of needing to perform forensic analysis? What are the defined RTOs and RPOs? How do they test their breach response procedures? What is their breach notification time to EEI? Is there ever a case where they would not report a personal data breach to EEI? What are the data protection laws in their countries for breach notification? What is the role of law enforcement in their countries in responding to a breach?

For the legal and breach notification process, Dieter would need to ascertain which breach notification regimes apply beyond the GDPR. To respond within the required time frames, what procedures do the processors have to ensure the notify EEI without undue delay? What information do they provide to EEI? How does EEI determine if there is a risk to the rights and freedoms of data subjects sufficient to report the breach to a DPA? How does DPA acquire the necessary information to send the DPA? Which DPAs is EEI required to report this to? What role does law enforcement play in the data breach response? Given the vast number of data subjects across the world EEI holds personal data on, there should be a list of all relevant DPAs and law enforcement agencies to be notified that Dieter can verify.

How does EEI determine if there is a high risk to the rights and freedoms of data subjects sufficient to report the breach to data subjects? What medium would EEI use to report to data subjects? How does EEI acquire the necessary information to send to the data subjects? How are the public relations aspects handled for the breach? When does outside counsel become involved with a personal data breach at EEI or one of its processors? Dieter will note from the recent breach that only subscribers were notified and not other potentially impacted individuals (e.g., referred friends who did not become subscribers). The determination process of who was notified and why should be examined.

7.2.5 Data Transfers

7.2.5.1 BCRs

EEI needs to have a set of binding corporate rules for its personal data transfers from the EEA that stay within its corporate group. These rules must contain the information described in Chapter 6, including the description of the personal data that is transferred, the types of data subjects involved, and the types and nature of the processing on the personal data. A description of how compliance with these rules observing the data protection principles and data subject rights are complied with and what the role of the DPO is in monitoring this compliance. Also, liability for noncompliance needs to be established, as well as EU entities acceptance of liability for non-EU entities rule breaches.

The rules must also list the third countries involved, so Dieter must compare a list of legal entities within the corporate group against the third countries listed in the rules. There should be a statement of how laws from these third countries might impact enforcing the DP principles and data subject rights. He must also review how adherence to the rules is independently audited within the group and any audit reports produced. EEI would be subject to the BCR-Controllers, and Dieter should refer to the recent WP29 table of the elements that these BCRs should contain. Within the two processors used by EEI, they may use subprocessors within the same corporate group and so be subject to the BCR-Processors, so Dieter should inquire about that with the processors and their adherence to the recent WP29 table of the elements (see Chapter 6). Finally, Dieter should review the DPAs approval of all applicable BCRs.

7.2.5.2 SCCs

EEI needs to enter into to controller-processor agreements for its personal data transfers from the EEA that go outside its corporate group. They are for transfers to its data mirroring and business continuity vendor in the Philippines (QuikBakk) and its Indian processor for software application development (Hyperbad). Hyperbad may only receive personal data periodically to be used to test software application changes, while QuikBakk would receive the full amount of personal data, given its role is providing a data mirroring service and the ability to provide a seamless backup website that could handle customer business if there are any service interruptions with the primary websites or other corporate services. Dieter should inquire as to why the personal data used for application testing was not at least pseudonymized and why real data records must be used.

Besides reviewing the controller-processor provisions as described in Chapter 3, Dieter should determine whether the agreement contains the standard contractual clauses (SCCs) for transferring data outside the EEA. He should ascertain which type (Type I or Type II) is being used and that it is the SCCs for transfers from an EU controller to non-EEA processors. All relevant sections should have been fully completed, and no sections should be missing, as it must follow the SCC exactly. It is important to ensure the rigorous description of the categories of personal data and purposes for the transfer and to match this against the processing that is evidenced in the data and processing inventory. The data subjects' third-party beneficiary rights are very important and should be noted. Any commercial clauses that have been added should be reviewed, as well. Dieter should review Philippine and Indian data protection law introduced in Chapter 6 and described in the companion book to understand if there are similar protections under those laws, if there are any data localization requirements, if there are any restrictions on moving data of certain types freely outside the country, and the powers of the local DPAs to assist if security incidents or other issues were to arise.

With these activities, Dieter and Helen have now performed an initial high-level assessment of EEI's compliance with the GDPR, including InfoSec and data breach assessments and data transfer mechanisms and so can make their report to establish a baseline level of GDPR compliance. They should have discussed remediations as they went along, training the various owners and specialists how to be compliant and prepared them for future audits where they will need to see not only policies, procedures, and contractual provisions, but also documented evidence of the effectiveness of the various measures to demonstrate the organization's compliance with GDPR and all relevant statutes and policies. Dieter and Helen must stay involved with all aspect of data protection, including new risks, while continuing to monitor for compliance with the GDPR and handling data subject inquiries regarding their DP rights and freedoms.

APPENDIX A

Various Topics for DPOs

Outsourcing Your DPO: Real-Life Scenarios

Once the necessary data protection officer skills are identified, the specific DPO is chosen, and the DPO services contract agreed upon with the controller/processor, the DPO can begin to undertake the tasks specified under Article 39 of the GDPR. In performing the outsourced DPO role, lots of interesting questions can arise concerning how various data protection scenarios will be evaluated under the GDPR. Given that no one has definitive answers yet, it is useful to examine all angles.

The following are four actual anonymized issues that have arisen in the outsourced DPO role.

Vulnerability Testing

Any company with a website or app should have vulnerability testing performed on that website/app to enhance its security. The question is whether the firm providing vulnerability/penetration testing services is a processor/subprocessor requiring a GDPR-compliant agreement? When firms are hired to test web-facing applications and websites to find weaknesses, they use a variety of techniques to search for existing and potential vulnerabilities. These include performing tests to identify weaknesses, such as buffer overflow and SQL injection, security misconfigurations, insecure authentication and access controls, and cross-site scripting. Any of these and other application and system configuration vulnerabilities, alone or in combination, could result in an unauthorized disclosure of personal data, triggering the duties under

Articles 33 and 34.

The vulnerability testing firm would then seem to be a processor/subprocessor operating under the instructions of the controller, despite the very limited likelihood they will gain access to personal data. This would trigger their Article 28 processor duties and the need for a GDPR controller-processor agreement. On one hand, the likelihood of them accessing personal data is very small — and it is not their intention to process any personal data, just identify vulnerabilities. On the other hand, the attempt to find vulnerabilities could always lead to the possible disclosure of personal data.

Is any entity that has a chance of processing personal data therefore at least a processor? Or does the likelihood need to exceed 50 percent? What is the role of intent, despite its absence from the definition of processing under Article 4(2)? Does the encryption of the personal data or its type and quantity impact the analysis? How about the types of vulnerability testing scans being done or the level of coding standard (e.g., OWASP ASVS) or information-security standard (e.g., ISO 27001) achieved on the code/system being scanned? The takeaway? The easiest solution may be to always consider any vulnerability testing firm requiring a processing agreement.

Photographic Images

Photographs are used all over the web from social media to advertising but may fall into a special category of personal data if they are used to authentication and identification and are processed by technical means. Exactly what type of "technical means" used for authentication and identification change a photographic image from personal data to biometric data?

Under existing data protection law, photographic images appear to be considered a form of biometric data. For example, in the *Willems* case,[1] the CJEU identified a facial image as biometric data, citing Reg. No. 2251/2004, which states that "biometric identifiers [facial images and fingerprints] should be integrated in the passport or travel document in order to establish a reliable link between the genuine holder and the document."

---

[1] W. P. Willems and Others v. Burgemeester van Nuth and Others, No. C-446/12 (CJEU Apr. 2015).

However, under the GDPR, Recital 51 states that photographs should not automatically be considered biometric data unless they are "processed through a specific technical means." Biometric data is a special category of data requiring extra protections defined in Article 4(14) as "personal data resulting from specific technical processing related to physical, physiological, or behavioral characteristics of a natural person, which allow for or confirm the unique identification of the natural person such as facial images or dactyloscopic data."

An example of specific technical means could be the explanation given in the Working Party's WP192 document,[2] which identifies the steps in facial recognition to include acquisition of a digital image, face detection, feature extraction, and comparison. Seeing this as a continuum, "technical means" could be considered any step after acquisition of a digital image. If the authentication and identification process using the digital image is performed by a person instead of purely technical means, does that mean the photo is not considered biometric data? If that person uses computer software to help enlarge or sharpen an image, are those to be considered to be technical means and then the photo is considered biometric data?

This topic needs further clarification from DPAs as to where the boundaries are and special focus for companies using digital images for identification and authentication on the type of processes they use.

Unified Consent

Consent is required to be able to load an app onto a mobile device and then get information from it, but this can lead to lots of requests for consent. Unifying these requests allows the user to more efficiently start using the app. In practical terms, how is unified consent achieved for installing an app on a device, accessing information on the device, and collecting and processing personal data? Under the GDPR, consent (assuming consent is the legal basis for processing) is required to be unbundled and granular, meaning that consent must be separately obtained from other terms and conditions and for each category of data. Under the ePrivacy Directive Article 5(3), consent must be obtained to first load an app on a device and then to access information (not just personal data) on the device.

---

2 Art. 29 DP WP, Op. 02/2012 on facial recognition in online and mobile services (March 2012).

Assume that a mobile device app will collect the name and health data of the individual. This means that there are four different types of consent in play: that to install the app; to access information on the device; to process the personal data (the user's name); and to process the special category of personal data (the user's health data). How should the requests for consent to each of these distinct consent requirements be presented — as one, two, three, or four requests — considering the information that must be presented for each consent would be somewhat different? How would this change if the app is gathering information from the mobile device itself, such as device or location information or the user's contacts? Balance is important, so the required informed consents are gathered with the least amount of disturbance to the app user's experience, perhaps through the use of layered privacy notices.

App Developer

Many app developers will use an app for their own purposes and so be considered a controller under the GDPR. But when might an app developer not be a controller? The test is, of course, that the controller determines the purposes (why) and means (how) of processing. When an app developer collects personal data for their own use, including information provided by the device, they would be considered a controller. But what about when the app collects personal data that will be used by another firm setting the rules for personal data collection and use? The second firm is clearly a controller, and the app developer seems like a processor acting under the instructions of the controller.

The Working Party's WP 169[3] states that "A processor could operate further to general guidance provided mainly on purposes and not going very deep in details with regard to means." As a controller determines the purposes and means, the question then becomes what are "means"? Referring to the history of the DPD, "means" is a shortened designation that "does not only refer to the technical ways of processing personal data, but also to the 'how' of processing, which includes questions like 'which data shall be processed,' 'which third parties shall have access to this data,' 'when data shall data be deleted,' etc."

---

[3] Art. 29 DP WP, Op. 1/2010 on the concepts of "controller" and "processor" (Feb. 2010).

Therefore, any processor determining these essential elements of the means would be classified as a controller, but not if merely determining the technical and organizational means of processing. Applying these definitions to the design and development of application software, would not designing code fall into the category of "means," as at a minimum the app developer is determining which data is processed and possibly how long it is kept? This is regardless of whether the app processes this data collected only for others.

The Working Party's WP202[4] states that app developers "have the greatest control over the precise manner in which the processing is undertaken." Or does the controller, in deciding which app to purchase and implement, make this decision about which personal data to gather based upon which app it deploys? Are app developers always at least joint controllers with those organizations that use their apps? If so, issues like who provides the Article 13 information to the data subject and contractual apportionment of liability and controller responsibilities become pertinent.

Subject Access Requests Under the GDPR — Uses in Litigation

Under the forthcoming General Data Protection Regulation, data subjects have a right to access their personal data held by a controller. Controllers under the GDPR will need to respond to data subjects who make a subject-access request. These rights currently exist under Data Protection Directive, Article 12, which requires controllers to confirm to a data subject if their personal data is being processed, the purposes of the processing, the categories of data being processed, and the recipients of that data, plus the logic on any automated processing decisions made on the basis of the personal data. Article 13 allows for certain restrictions on these rights under member state laws, including "for the protection of the data subject and of the rights and freedoms of others." GDPR Article 15 enhances these requirements by requiring the responses be within a month, generally without charge, and with additional information, such as data retention periods.

This seems simple enough, except for the possible increase in administrative work for data controllers.

---

4   Art. 29 DP WP, Op. 02/2013 on apps on smart devices (Feb. 2013).

Litigation complicates this relatively simple requirement. Although differing widely across EU jurisdictions, there are typically rights of disclosure or discovery by parties involved in litigation. For example, in the U.K., there is standard disclosure for both litigating parties to each other, and additional disclosures can be ordered by the court. Ireland has litigant-requested court-ordered discovery, while continental EU courts, under civil law, have varying levels of litigant-requested and court-initiated and ordered discovery. Discovery/Disclosure requests can overlap with SARs. Restricting access to personal data under SARs is the legal professional privilege, which protects communications and documents created for litigation or legal advice given. LPP is a combination of litigation privilege and legal advice privilege.

LPP is an allowable restriction to SARs under Directive Article 13 (GDPR Article 23). The Irish Data Protection Commissioner advises that individuals do not have a right to access information relating to them, which is subject to LPP in court. The U.K. Information Commissioner's Office states that personal data is exempt from the right of access if LPP can be claimed for it in legal proceedings. Problems can arise when parties use their access rights under EU privacy laws to attempt to circumvent LPP or other limitations on discovery/disclosure. Two recent cases in the U.K. and one from Ireland demonstrate this tension between the right of confidentiality for legal matters under LPP, discovery/disclosure litigation requests, and the right to access personal data via an SAR.

In the 2012 case of Dublin Bus,[5] the High Court of Ireland considered whether there was a right under the Data Protection Act, as asserted by the plaintiff and supported by the DPC, to receive certain personal data to support their litigation claims. The plaintiff had fallen on a bus and, after commencing litigation, asked under an SAR for the CCTV video of their fall. The defendant refused, stating the video was protected by litigation privilege. The DPC then issued an enforcement notice on the defendant to provide the video. The defendant appealed that because the motive of the plaintiff was to use the video for litigation purposes, the DPC was exercising the role of court-ordered discovery. The court ruled that this was actually a request concerning privacy rights, there was no statutory exception for refusing an SAR because the data would be used in litigation, and it was not its role to fashion such a new exception.

---

5 Dublin Bus v. Data Protection Commissioner, No. 339 (IEHC Aug. 2012).

In the 2017 case of Holyoake,[6] the High Court of England and Wales considered whether LPP can be used to hide a privacy violation or protect communications about responding to an SAR. The plaintiff's SAR was originally rejected on the grounds that it would be used to support litigation, the data could be obtained through the disclosure process, and a significant amount of personal data would be subject to litigation privilege but, after being narrowed, was carried out by the defendants. The court noted that while litigation privilege "arises where a document has been brought into existence for the sole or dominant purpose of use for litigation ... Litigation privilege may be ... disapplied where it [is] designed to act as a cloak for crime or fraud." The court ruled that a violation of privacy was not considered a crime or fraud that would result in the dis-applying of LPP to the SAR. It also ruled that the use of lawyers to conduct an SAR search allowed LPP to be used on communications about that search, even though non-lawyers could have conducted the search.

In the 2017 case of Dawson-Damer,[7] the Court of Appeals of England and Wales considered whether a litigation motive for an SAR under the Data Protection Act was a valid reason to reject it and also the jurisdictional scope of LPP under the DPA. The appellants had issued an SAR against the trustee of a foreign trust. The trustee, a law firm, resisted the SAR, stating that the personal data was covered by LPP, including the wider privilege of that foreign jurisdiction. The court of appeals ruled that SARs were not limited to simply verifying and correcting personal data and no other use, and so the motive for issuing an SAR was not relevant. The court also ruled that the LPP under the DPA was the privilege available under English — not foreign — law, as the DPD Article 13 restrictions allowed for national laws that applied only within their own jurisdictions.

The ICO's 2014 Subject Access Code of Practice addressed the SAR/LPP/discovery issues: "It has been suggested that case law provides authority for organisations to refuse to comply with an SAR where the requester is contemplating or has already begun legal proceedings. The Information Commissioner does not accept this view, but he recognises that: the courts have discretion as to whether or not to order compliance

---

6 Holyoake v. Candy, No. 52 (EWHC QB Jan. 2017).
7 Dawson-Damer v. Taylor Wessing LLP, No. 74 (EWCA Civ. Feb. 2017).

with an SAR; and if a court believes that the disclosure of information in connection with legal proceedings should, more appropriately, be determined by … the courts' rules on disclosure, it may refuse to order personal data to be disclosed … Nevertheless, simply because a court may choose not to order the disclosure of an individual's personal data does not mean that, in the absence of a relevant exemption, the DPA does not require you to disclose it. It simply means that the individual may not be able to enlist the court's support to enforce his or her right."

To summarize, the GDPR will bring certain enhancements to the requirements for controllers in handling SARs. Litigation, including the role of discovery/disclosure and LPP, can complicate the response to SARs. LPP can be a valid reason for controllers to decline to provide certain personal data requested by an SAR, but LPP only applies to personal data in documents and communications relating to legal advice and litigation. In absence of LPP or other legal restrictions such a national security, data subjects have a right to their personal data requested under an SAR, even if intending to use it in court against the defendant controller. Controllers should become familiar with all the restrictions allowed by their national laws in replying to an SAR and the GDPR's new SAR requirements.

Legal Response to Data Breaches in the Cloud

Cloud computing, as it moves closer to being a public utility like power and water, will be defined mostly by the risks involved. These include data privacy risks. As is often the case with new IT services riding a marketing boom, the risks of cloud computing tend to be minimized by the marketers. Yet, it is by understanding, assessing, and managing those risks that confidence in cloud computing can expand significantly, for both organizational and personal users of the cloud. Given the increasing deployment of bring your own device (BYOD) into the corporate space, the prior distinctions between organizational and individual data and process are becoming blurred, and thus the cloud risk evaluation process should be applicable to all types of users.

When evaluating the risks of cloud computing, organizations and individuals (hereafter, cloud consumers) need to take a hard look at both themselves and their cloud service providers (CSPs). Cloud consumers first need to understand how they organize and manage their confidential data, which then provides a foundation for assessing their CSPs. A standard methodology can be used in evaluating the risks for both cloud consumers and CSPs, whether the outsourcing is to private clouds, hybrid clouds, or public clouds and regardless of the service model(s) used. Cloud consumers will first need to understand all the types of cloud computing risk before being able to assess and manage the risk.

There are six major categories of cloud computing risk: legal, data protection, contracting, governance, verification, and response. Legal risk comes from the totality of all legal obligations that an organization has from all cloud-related statutes it is subject to globally. Data protection risk involves the design, implementation, and evaluation of safeguards by the cloud consumer and CSP to protect the privacy of data. Contracting risk is how well cloud consumers have legally protected themselves against undesirable cloud-related events. Governance risk looks at how interoperable data and process are and how portable they are to new CSPs. Verification risk comes from the comprehensiveness and quality of independent third-party assurances about the CSPs used. Response risk involves dealing with security-related incidents that impact the consumer's data privacy, including data breaches.

Privacy issues arise under both data protection risk and response risk. The protections to safeguard the privacy of data are well understood and not new with cloud computing, although they do reemphasize certain controls. For example, encryption is a must-have in the cloud computing world. Encryption must be deployed not only during transit from the cloud consumer to the CSP, but also while stored by the CSP on disk, in mirror sites, on backup tapes, etcetera, and in use, to the extent possible. Data protection risk has both a technical/process aspect and a legal aspect, in complying with a burgeoning number of general; i.e., reasonableness or specific; i.e., requiring information security policies, provisions in laws globally.

Similarly, response risk to a cloud data breach has both technical/process and legal aspects, plus an added dimension. The technical/process response includes how to identify that a security incident has occurred; how to quarantine the intrusion, repair infected systems and restore affected data; and how to undertake reviews and remediations to prevent recurrence. The added dimension is the business/reputational response, which tries to limit the impact on the entity's financial viability, revenue loss, and diminishing of trademarks and brand names. The legal response requires that organizations comply with a variety of statutory and regulatory requirements for notification, to get law enforcement and regulators involved, and for imaging or safeguarding potential evidence.

There are many different data breach notification laws globally, often part of the local privacy laws, and these are growing. It is important to remember that when cloud consumers enter the cloud, they have by default become global players, meaning that they will likely be subject to the data privacy laws of more than one country. In Europe, the ePrivacy Directive requires EU member states to implement local legislation for service providers responsible for hosting and transmitting consumers' data to notify the appropriate national authorities upon the event of a data breach. If consumers' data is breached and the breach could have a negative impact on the consumers, they must then also be notified.

While there is yet no general federal data breach notification requirement in the United States, there are sector-specific regulations in health care and financial services for reporting of data breaches. Also, there are general data breach notification laws in almost every state. These laws typically require notification to consumers if their data is breached, thereby exposing them to risk of harm. This is most typically the case when the data is personally identifiable information or financial information that is stored in an unencrypted format. What may vary between the different state statutes is the type of information that must be reported, to whom it must be reported, and when it must be reported. These laws are constantly changing, as several U.S. states, i.e., Connecticut and Vermont, have recently revised their data breach statutory requirements.

In the Asia-Pacific region, there are both voluntary guidelines and industry-specific requirements to report breaches. For example, Australia had no general data breach statute, but this has become mandatory. In Hong Kong, the proposed changes to the local privacy ordinance will make the breach notification process voluntary, but the government has promulgated guidelines and templates in advance of those changes. Japan has industry-sector regulations regarding data breach notification. In Taiwan and South Korea, newer revisions to privacy laws require data breach notifications. In China, local versions of data breach laws complement national breach notice regulations on service providers.

The legal response to a data breach when data is outsourced to the cloud essentially comes down to answering a series of questions:

- What data breach notification and privacy laws are implicated by a data breach at a CSP, given that the data servers and consumers may be situated in disparate countries around the world?
- Who is responsible for reporting a data breach: the CSP or the cloud consumer?
- When must the breach be reported—immediately, after an investigation, or perhaps never?
- To whom must the breach be reported: the local data protection authorities, industry regulators, local and/or international law enforcement, i.e., Interpol, Department of Justice agencies, and/or the data owners or their data custodians, if outsourced?
- In what circumstances must the data breach be reported, such as when a certain number of records or a certain type of sensitive data was breached or when criminal activity is suspected?
- What types of information must be reported?
- How does the CSP know, in a virtual-resource multitenant cloud environment, which cloud consumer's data has been breached?
- What type of evidence must be saved for future criminal investigations or civil litigation, i.e., network and system logs or data/system images, and how can this be done in a multitenant cloud environment?

This example guidance from the Hong Kong government provides some insight into part of the legal response. It suggests that the data custodian first gather information, including when and where the breach occurred, how it was detected, the cause, what type of personal data was affected, and the number of data subjects potentially impacted. It advises notifying data subjects when the "real risk of harm is reasonably foreseeable." In its breach notification, it suggests including the date and time of the breach and its discovery, the cause of the breach, the personal data breached, the potential risks of harm, the remedial measures to ensure no further data loss, a contact person and number, the law enforcement or other agencies notified, what is being done to assist affected consumers, and what they can do themselves to mitigate the risk of harm, such as identity theft and financial fraud.

With data breaches, all cloud consumers should take the approach that the question is not if they will happen but when—and will I be ready? Much like business continuity plans but with even less certainty as to timing, data breaches can and do occur, and to some of the best-known brand names and organizations, even those with a strong public internet security profile. CSPs, by centralizing cloud consumers' data, are a target for bad actors, so cloud consumers should create and test a robust response plan to use when the data breach event occurs, and the privacy of their cloud-based data is compromised. This plan should address all three areas of cloud data breach response, as explained above, including the legal aspects. Only then can cloud consumers confidently expand their footprint in the cloud.

Consent to Children's Data — Is It Legal?

Special events involving children are highly sought after by children and parents alike. Especially those that involve going through an assessment process to be selected for something as prestigious as national science fairs, debate contests, math competitions, coding conferences, or programs taught at prestigious schools and universities. Parents and children alike are proud to be among those who get invited. It is then very disappointing, after the child has already been chosen, to be presented with a "consent" form that the parent must sign for the child to further participate in the desired program.

These forms typically combine several different rights together when seeking a single consent. Typical are those forms asking for consent to use a child's personal data and image and consent to the ownership of any intellectual property generated by the child's participation in the program. Worse, the intended processing of personal data requires that the parent agree to allow images taken of their child during the program to be permanently retained and used on social media and websites for the program's publicity. The right to not consent along with alternative ways to participate is never provided and the right to withdraw consent is not stated.

Based on reading these "consent" forms, they would appear to violate the Data Protection Directive and the General Data Protection

Regulation, which require consent to be unambiguous, specific, informed, and freely given to be valid. In these cases, consent cannot be freely given, due to the coercive nature of the form's wording and the process of obtaining consent. As such, gathering consent in such a manner and the subsequent processing of the children's personal data would be illegal.

The Law

Consent is required to be freely given to valid. The WP29 WP187[8] states that "Consent can only be valid if the data subject is able to exercise a real choice, and there is no risk of deception, intimidation, coercion or significant negative consequences if he/she does not consent. If the consequences of consenting undermine individuals' freedom of choice, consent would not be free."

WP29 WP131[9] states that "free consent means a voluntary decision, by an individual in possession of all of his faculties, taken in the absence of coercion of any kind, be it social, financial, psychological or other. Any consent given under the threat of non-treatment or lower quality treatment in a medical situation cannot be considered as 'free' ... Reliance on consent should be confined to cases where the individual data subject has a genuine free choice and is subsequently able to withdraw the consent without detriment."

Because valid consent is not possible where significant negative consequences like non-participation are present, the data controllers must find their legal basis elsewhere or provide a valid method of consent. WP187 makes it clear that if consent is initially asked for but another legal basis is used, then "doubts could be raised as to the original use of consent as the initial legal ground: if the processing could have taken place from the beginning using this other ground, presenting the individual with a situation where he is asked to consent to the processing could be considered as misleading or inherently unfair."

In addition, the ability to withdraw consent is required. As WP187 states, "In principle, consent can be considered to be deficient if no effective withdrawal is permitted."

---

8 Art. 29 DP WP, Op. 15/2011 on the definition of consent (July 2011).
9 Art. 29 DP WP, Working Document on the processing of personal data relating to health in electronic health records (EHR) (Feb. 2007).

The situation of a child and their parent being forced to consent or lose the ability to participate is similar to that of an employee. As described in WP29 WP48,[10] "where consent is required from a worker, and there is a real or potential relevant prejudice that arises from not consenting, the consent is not valid in terms of satisfying either Article 7 or Article 8 as it is not freely given. If it is not possible for the worker to refuse it is not consent.... An area of difficulty is where the giving of consent is a condition of employment. The worker is in theory able to refuse consent, but the consequence may be the loss of a job opportunity. In such circumstances consent is not freely given and is therefore not valid."

WP29 WP259[11] further clarifies prior guidance, noting, "The concept of consent as used in the Data Protection Directive… has evolved. The GDPR provides further clarification and specification of the requirements for obtaining and demonstrating valid consent." And, "If consent is bundled up as a non-negotiable part of terms and conditions it is presumed not to have been freely given. Accordingly, consent will not be considered to be free if the data subject is unable to refuse or withdraw his or her consent without detriment. The notion of imbalance between the controller and the data subject is also taken into consideration by the GDPR."

GDPR Recital 38 states, "Such specific protection should, in particular, apply to the use of personal data of children for the purposes of marketing." The emotional aspects for children and their parents are described in this statement from WP187: "While a situation of subordination is often the main reason preventing consent to be free, other contextual elements can influence the decision of the data subject. They can have for instance a financial dimension, or an emotional or a practical dimension."

The Forms

These forms typically demand consent as a prerequisite for further participation but offer no alternative manner for a child to participate in the program if refusing to consent to having their image captured

---

10 Art. 29 DP WP, Op. 8/2001 on the processing of personal data in the employment context (Sept. 2001).
11 Art. 29 DP WP, Guidelines on Consent under Regulation 2016/679 (Nov. 2017).

and processed online. None of the main activities of the children's participation has anything to do with the capture of their images. The images of these children instead are not only captured but then further processed by posting on publicly available social media and websites. What happens to the images of children on the internet when bad actors intervene is well known enough. There should always be a more granular ability to restrict the use of a child's images to a less durable medium, such as broadcast television, printed newspapers, or Snapchat-like capabilities while withholding consent to other more durable mediums, such as social media, video portals, and other websites.

Parents should be able to withhold consent entirely to processing of the images of their child online, when that processing is not strictly necessary as part of the principal activity the children are involved in. Differentiation should also be made of photos of individual children or close-ups and photos of large groups of children or crowd scenes and also for labels naming the child or their school and unlabeled photos. Videos that depict any child individually should require separate consent, given the additional invasive properties of video and any audio recorded should be strictly necessary for participation in the program. The consent forms combine IP and personal data into a single consent, contrary to the GDPR requirement that they be properly unbundled. The forms also do not provide notification of the ability to withdraw consent previously granted.

Conclusion

I contend that this coerced and therefore illegal consent may be the most widespread data protection problem today. So, what exactly are the DPAs doing about it? Has anyone seen a specific instance of their DPA educating controllers or starting enforcement actions based upon coerced consent of parents regarding processing of their children's personal data? The GDPR requires in Article 57(1)(b) that DPAs have as one of their tasks "Activities addressed specifically to children shall receive specific attention." I asked my local DPA to educate specific controllers on this and the controllers promised to do something, but not until next year. When will all DPAs across the EU start educating and investigating controllers about these widespread violations of consent to the processing of children's personal data?

EU Data Transfers to the U.S. — Model Clauses but Why?

The so-called Schrems II case for possible referral to the CJEU makes for fascinating reading. This unintended attack on the standard contractual clauses (SCC) mechanism may turn out to be a legally moot, as it addresses decisions made under the expiring DPD and the GDPR allows DPAs and the EC to fashion such model clauses. However, it does have the potential to impact the credibility of this second of three often-used mechanisms for transferring personal data from the EU to the U.S. In reading though this lengthy opinion, two questions that I have long ruminated on started to resonate again. Specifically, why does the personal data of any EU resident ever need to leave the EEA? And why does the EC keep supporting relatively weak data protection mechanisms, such as the Safe Harbor, the Privacy Shield, and SCCs?

Before discussing the case, it is important to understand what it analyzes and what it does not analyze. It does analyze the ability of EU data subjects to seek judicial recourse against the U.S. government in case of abuses by U.S. intelligence agencies. What it does not analyze is the totality of U.S. privacy law protections, which encompass more than just federal statutes and regulations. State law privacy statutes and the common law are very significant sources of privacy protections, as is case law, especially class action litigation. This is not well understood in the EU, who are more familiar with being protected by a comprehensive data protection statute and having to parse reams of case law and many sectoral statutes is not a common experience.

In a 153-page decision[12] (U.K. and Irish judges write some very long opinions), the high court of Ireland went through an exhaustive look at applicable EU and national laws that protected the rights of Irish data subjects (although Schrems is Austrian, he filed suit in Ireland, the EU headquarters for Facebook, the ultimate target of his requests to the DPC). The court then undertook an even more exhaustive analysis of U.S. privacy law, focusing specifically on those laws allowing the intelligence agencies to parse the personal data of EU data subjects. It looked to the protections that those EU data subjects would have in the case of U.S. intelligence agency overreach. Given that the U.S.

---

12 DPC v. Facebook and Schrems, No. 2016 No. 4809 (IEHC Comm. Oct. 2017).

government was one of four amicus curiae invited by the court, it can only be assumed its positions were well represented.

The court's review of EU data protection focused on Article 47 of the EU Charter of Fundamental Rights. This provides the right to an effective remedy when those rights have been violated, in a fair, timely, and public hearing before an independent and impartial tribunal. The data protection and privacy rights of EU citizens are declared in the charter, the Council of Europe's Convention on Human Rights, and the Treaty on the Functioning of the EU, as well as the DPD. But these only go so far, as both the Treaty on the EU and the DPD make it clear that matters of national security are for the individual member states and processing of personal data for national security does not fall under the DPD.

The complaint to the DPC, which had to be reformulated after the Schrems I CJEU judgment[13] invalidated the Safe Harbor decision, requested the DPC to suspend data flows from Facebook in Ireland to Facebook in the U.S., primarily due to deficiencies in the SCCs used and secondarily because of mass surveillance by intelligence agencies of Facebook-held data. The DPC reformulated this to be a review of the adequacy of U.S. privacy law for EU data subjects and the ability of SCCs like Facebook's to offer adequate protections. The DPC investigation found remedies for EU data subjects to be fragmentary and the standing requirement before U.S. federal courts a major impediment in obtaining relief for intelligence agency activities. Because SCCs only provide a cause of action against the data exporter and importer but not the U.S. government, they do not remedy this deficiency.

Facebook argued that as this processing was for purposes of national security, it was outside the scope of the DPD and processing of EU member states for national security[14] should be compared against processing in the U.S. for national security. The court disagreed for many reasons, including that as all transfers to third countries could subsequently be subject to processing by intelligence agencies, the DPD (or GDPR) would never apply to such transfers and recent CJEU's caselaw stated that all personal data transfers to intelligence agencies are done under the DPD. Facebook also contended that the Privacy Shield decision was an adequacy decision by the EC, and any referral to the

---

13 Schrems v. DPC, No. C362/14 (CJEU Oct. 2015).
14 *See e.g.*, Netherlands, Wet op de inlichtingen en veiligheidsdiensten (July 2017).

CJEU on SCCs would be a collateral attack on the Privacy Shield. The court disagreed, noting that the Privacy Shield was not an adequacy decision on the U.S. privacy regime but instead a unique mechanism allowing personal data transfers by organizations meeting the specific requirements of the Privacy Shield.

The court then analyzed the SCCs, focusing just on the controller-processor SCCs used by Facebook.[15] It noted that the third-party beneficiary clause, which allows a data subject to bring suit against the two parties (data exporter and importer) to the contract for violations of their respective obligations, excludes suit against the EU-based data exporter for not complying with EU data protection law. The DPC asserted that the SCCs do not provide the high level of protection for the personal data of EU data subjects that they would receive within the EU. The court agreed that SCCs by themselves to not provide a high level of protection and that, while it was within the existing powers of DPAs to prevent data flows to countries it determined to not be providing sufficient protections, doing so without coordination among all EU member state DPAs might prove problematic.

The court then analyzed U.S. privacy law in regards to processing by intelligence agencies. The DPC had only looked at whether an EU citizen had an Article 47 right, while the U.S. government and Facebook insisted U.S. laws and practices must be reviewed holistically. After looking at FISA orders, the Patriot Act, and Executive Order 13233, the court focused primarily on programs operating under FISA §702, PRISM and Upstream and found that there was "mass indiscriminate processing of data" by the surveillance agencies. The court also found that the Fourth Amendment protections against government surveillance were not available to most EU citizens. The court reviewed ECPA, the Privacy Act/Judicial Redress Act (which the NSA is exempted from), and the Administrative Procedure Act for possible remedies without being reassured due to various restrictions but was most concerned about the federal court (Article III) standing requirement.

---

15 Commission Decision of 5 Feb. 2010 on standard contractual clauses for the transfer of personal data to processors established in third countries under Directive 95/46/EC of the European Parliament and of the Council, revised by Commission Implementing Decision (EU) 2016/2297 of 16 December 2016 amending Decisions 2001/497/EC and 2010/87/EU on standard contractual clauses for the transfer of personal data to third countries and to processors established in such countries, under Directive 95/46/EC of the European Parliament and of the Council.

Due to the lack of notification when subject to surveillance, the court did not believe an EU plaintiff could plead sufficient injury for standing purposes. While it noted there were various procedures to prevent misuse of data, this was "not the same as of providing a remedy where the rules are broken and data is unlawfully collected." The DPC also asserted that the Privacy Shield ombudsman role, which oversees all personal data transferred from the EU to the U.S. under any of the available mechanisms, was not independent of the executive, was not a permanent position established in law, and had no judicial oversight. The Article 29 Working Party largely echoed these same concerns in its more recent review of the Privacy Shield.[16] The high court sided with the DPC on the need to refer the question of the adequacy of SCCs to the CJEU and would formulate the questions to submit.

Returning to my original questions, why does the personal data of any EU resident ever need to leave the EEA? Previously, all processing for a global organization might need to be done centrally at its main data center in the U.S., but that is no longer the case with significant data center and distributed processing capabilities available across the EU. Any U.S. company wanting to transfer personal data from the EU to the U.S. should therefore be required to meet a significant necessity threshold before being allowed to undertake such transfers. Typical corporate reasons, such as economic efficiency, marketing plans, or data analytics, would not meet this necessity threshold to transfer personal data outside the EEA.

Why does the EC keep supporting relatively weak privacy mechanisms, such as Safe Harbor, Privacy Shield, and SCCs? There are ample rigorous certification mechanisms available in information security, privacy, and data protection, so U.S. companies who meet the necessity threshold should then be required to be independently certified in data protection/security and annually re-certified. The GDPR's new certification mechanism may be of use here. Data transferred only when necessary and under independent certification would minimize the amount of EU personal data available to U.S. intelligence agencies and would be a significant improvement in assurance over the Privacy Shield and SCCs.

---

16 Art. 29 DP WP, EU — U.S. Privacy Shield — First annual Joint Review (Nov. 2017).

APPENDIX B

Table of Authorities

Cases

Bayerisches Landesamt für Datenschutzaufsicht, Datenschutzbeauftragter darf keinen Interessenkonflikten unterliegen (Oct. 2016)................17

Dawson-Damer v. Taylor Wessing LLP, No. 74 (EWCA Civ. Feb. 2017).........185

DPC v. Facebook and Schrems, No. 2016 No. 4809 (IEHC Comm., Oct. 2017)..194

Dublin Bus v. Data Protection Commissioner, No. 339 (IEHC Aug. 2012).....184

Holyoake v. Candy, No. 52 (EWHC QB, Jan. 2017)..........................185

Schrems v. DPC, No. C362/14 (CJEU Oct. 2015)............................195

W. P. Willems and Others v. Burgemeester van Nuth and Others, No. C-446/12 (CJEU Apr. 2015)..180

Statutes

5 U.S.C. § 552a(d)-(e)...102

Commission Decision 2001/497/EC of 15 June 2001 on standard contractual clauses for the transfer of personal data to third countries, under Directive 95/46/EC..141

Commission Decision 2004/915/EC of 27 Dec. 2004 amending Decision 2001/497/EC as regards the introduction of an alternative set of standard contractual clauses for the transfer of personal data to third countries............141

Commission Decision of 5 Feb. 2010 on standard contractual clauses for the transfer of personal data to processors established in third countries under Directive 95/46/EC of the European Parliament and of the Council, revised by Commission Implementing Decision (EU) 2016/2297 of 16 December 2016 amending Decisions 2001/497/EC and 2010/87/EU on standard contractual clauses for the transfer of personal data to third countries and to processors established in such countries, under Directive 95/46/EC of the European Parliament and of the Council..............196

Commission Implementing Decision (EU) 2016/1250 of 12 July 2016 pursuant to Directive 95/46/EC of the European Parliament and of the Council on the adequacy of the protection provided by the EU-U.S. Privacy Shield (notified under document C(2016) 4176)............................140

Commission Implementing Decision of 21 Aug. 2012 pursuant to Directive 95/46/EC of the European Parliament and of the Council on the adequate protection of personal data by the Eastern Republic of Uruguay with regard to automated process of personal data. 139

Directive 2002/58/EC of the European Parliament and of the Council of 12 July 2002 concerning the processing of personal data and the protection of privacy in the electronic communications sector (Directive on privacy and electronic communications), as modified by 2009/132/EC..............66

Directive 95/46/EC of the European Parliament and of the Council of 24 October 1995 on the protection of individuals with regard to the processing of personal data and on the free movement of such data (DPD)............4

ETS No. 108 (Jan. 1981)..139

EU Data Protection Directive, Directive 95/46/EC of the European Parliament and of the Council of 24 4

Federal Information Security Management Act, 44 U.S.C. § 3542 (2002)....112

Netherlands, Wet op de inlichtingen en veiligheidsdiensten (July 2017)....195

Pub. L. 107-347 (Dec. 2002)...102

Regulation (EU) 2016/679 of the European Parliament and of the Council of 27 April 2016 on the protection of natural persons with regard to the processing of personal data and on the free movement of such data, and repealing Directive 95/46/EC (General Data Protection Regulation). 2

Guidance

AIPCA/CAC, Generally Accepted Privacy Principles 76

Art. 29 DP WP, Adequacy Referential (Feb. 2018). 138

Art. 29 DP WP, EU — U.S. Privacy Shield — First annual Joint Review (Nov. 2017)..197

Art. 29 DP WP, Guidelines for identifying a controller or processor's lead supervisory authority, r1 (Apr. 2017). 62

Art. 29 DP WP, Guidelines on Automated individual decision-making and Profiling for the purposes of Regulation 2016/679, r1 (Feb. 2018). 59

Art. 29 DP WP, Guidelines on Consent under Regulation 2016/679 (Nov. 2017)..53

Art. 29 DP WP, Guidelines on Data Protection Impact Assessment (DPIA) and determining whether processing is "likely to result in a high risk" for the purposes of Regulation 2016/679, r1 (Oct. 2017). 96

Art. 29 DP WP, Guidelines on Data Protection Officers ("DPOs") r1 (Apr. 2017). 12

Art. 29 DP WP, Guidelines on Personal data breach notification under Regulation 2016/679, r1 (Feb. 2018). 61, 118

Art. 29 DP WP, Guidelines on the right to data portability, r1 (Apr. 2017). 59

Art. 29 DP WP, Guidelines on transparency under Regulation 2016/679 (Nov. 2017)..56

Art. 29 DP WP, Working Document on the processing of personal data relating to health in electronic health records (EHR) (Feb. 2007)................191

Art. 29 DP WP, Working Document setting up a table with the elements and principles to be found in binding corporate rules (updated) (Feb. 2018)..143

Art. 29 DP WP, Working Document setting up a table with the elements and principles to be found in Processor binding corporate rules (updated) (Feb. 2018)..143

CEN, Personal Data Protection Audit Framework (EU Directive EC 95.46) — *Part I: Baseline Framework and* Part II: Checklists, questionnaires and templates for users of the framework solution........................76

CNIL, analys d'impact sur la protection de donnees (Dec. 2017). 101

CNIL, Measures for the Privacy Risk Treatment (June 2012). 100

CNIL, Methodology (how to carry out a PIA) (June 2015)..................100

CNIL, Règlement européen sur la protection des données personnelles – Guide du sous-traitant (Sept. 2017).................................68

CNIL, Tools (templates and knowledge bases) (June 2015). 100

DPC, Guide to Audit Process v2.0 (Aug. 2014)...........................76

EC, Guide to the EY-U.S. Privacy Shield (Aug. 2016). 140

EDPS, Position paper on the role of Data Protection Officers in ensuring effective compliance with Regulation (EC) 45/2001 (Nov. 2005). 65

EDPS, Professional Standards for Data Protection Officers of the EU institutions and bodies working under Regulation (EC) 45/2001 (Oct. 2010). 65

ENISA, Data breach notifications in the EU (Jan. 2011). 118

ENISA, Online privacy tools for the general public — Towards a methodology for the evaluation of PETs for internet and mobile users (Dec. 2015) . . .134

ENISA, PETs controls matrix — A systematic approach for assessing online and mobile privacy tools (Dec. 2016). 134

ENISA, Privacy and Data Protection by Design — from policy to engineering (Dec. 2014). 133

ENISA, Privacy by design in big data — An overview of privacy enhancing technologies in the era of big data analytics (Dec. 2015). 133

ENISA, Privacy Enhancing Technologies: Evolution and State of the Art — A Community Approach to PETs Maturity Assessment (Dec. 2016). 134

ENISA, Readiness Analysis for the Adoption and Evolution of Privacy Enhancing Technologies Methodology, Pilot Assessment, and Continuity Plan (Dec. 2015) 134

ENISA, Recommendations for a methodology of the assessment of severity of personal data breaches (Dec. 2013). 126

ENISA, Recommendations on European Data Protection Certification (Nov. 2017). 78

ENISA, Recommendations on technical implementation guidelines (Apr. 2012). 126

ICO, Auditing data protection — a guide to ICO data protection audits v.3.5 (June 2015). 77

ICO, Conducting privacy impact assessments code of practice (Feb. 2014). 99

ICO, GDPR guidance: Contracts and liabilities between controllers and processors (Sept. 2017). 70

ISACA, IS Audit/Assurance Program — Data Privacy. 76

ISO/IEC 29134:2017, Information technology — Security techniques — Guidelines for privacy impact assessment (June 2017). 103

OMB Mem. M-03-22, Guidance for Implementing the Privacy Provisions of the E-Government Act (Sept. 2003). 102

Ontario IPC, Privacy and Security by Design: A Convergence of Paradigms (Jan. 2013). 132

Ontario IPC, Privacy and Security by Design: An Enterprise Architecture Approach (Sept. 2013). 132

Ontario IPC, Privacy by Design (rev. Sept. 2013). 127

Ontario IPC, Privacy by Design in Law, Policy and Practice: A White Paper for Regulators, Decision-makers and Policy-makers (Aug. 2011). 132

Ontario IPC, Privacy by Design: In the Age of Big Data (June 2012). 130

Ontario IPC, Privacy by Design: From Policy to Practice (Sept. 2011). 130

Ontario IPC, Privacy Engineering: Proactively Embedding Privacy, by Design (Jan. 2014). 129

Ontario IPC, The Roadmap for Privacy by Design in Mobile Communications: A Practical Tool for Developers, Service Providers, and Users (Dec. 2010). 131

OPC, Privacy Enhancing Technologies — A Review of Tools and Techniques (Nov. 2017). 135

U.S. Department of Homeland Security, Privacy Impact Assessment for ECS (Jan. 2013). 102

U.S. Department of Homeland Security, Privacy Threshold Analysis (Sept. 2015). 102

Standards

AEPC, Esquema de certificación de Delegados de Protección de Datos, r1.1 (Oct. 2017). 13

FIPS, Pub. 199, Standards for Security Categorization of Federal Information and Information Systems (Feb. 2004). 112

ISO Guide 73, Risk management — Vocabulary (Nov. 2009). 82

ISO/IEC 27001:2013, Information technology — Security techniques — Information security management systems — Requirements (Oct. 2013). 107

ISO/IEC 27002:2013, Information Technology — Security Techniques — Code of Practice for Information Security Controls (Oct. 2013). 109

ISO/IEC 27005:2008, Information technology — Security techniques — Information security risk management (June 2008). 83

ISO/IEC 27005:2011, Information technology — Security techniques — Information security risk management (June 2011).....................83

ISO/IEC 29000:2011, Information technology — Security Techniques — Privacy framework (Dec. 2011). 112

ISO/IEC 29151:2017, Information technology — Security Techniques — Code of practice for personally identifiable information protection (Aug. 2017)..111

NIST, SP 800-37 r2 (draft), Risk Management Framework for Information Systems and Organizations (Sept. 2017).............................113

NIST, SP 800-53 r5 (draft), Security and Privacy Controls for Information Systems and Organizations (Aug. 2017).............................113

NIST, SP 800-53A r4, Assessing Security and Privacy Controls in Federal Information Systems and Organizations (Dec. 2014). 113

Opinions

Art. 29 DP WP Op. 8/2001 on the processing of personal data in the employment context (Sept. 2001)...................................192

Art. 29 DP WP, Op. 02/2012 on facial recognition in online and mobile services..181

Art. 29 DP WP, Op. 02/2013 on apps on smart devices (Feb. 2013)..........183

Art. 29 DP WP, Op. 1/2010 on the concepts of "controller" and "processor" (Feb. 2010)... 46, 182

Art. 29 DP WP, Op. 15/2011 on the definition of consent (July 2011). 191

Art. 29 DP WP, Op. 2/2017 on data processing at work (June 2017). 65

Art. 29 DP WP, Op. 3/2013 on purpose limitation (Apr. 2013)................48

Art. 29 DP WP, Op. 5/2014 on Anonymisaton Techniques (Apr. 2014) 116

Art. 29 DP WP, Op. 6/2014 on the notion of legitimate interests of the data controller under Article 7 of Directive 95/46/EC (Apr. 2014). 52